# Turmeric & Spice

## Indian Cuisine for the Mind, Body, and Spirit

### Bina Mehta

**bina**
MEHTA

seek a truer you

Published 2018 in the United States by
TruerU Ink
1520 S. College Ave.
Fort Collins, CO 80524
(970) 444-2462
www.TruerUInk.com

Editors: Wordwise Editing, Your Editor On Call
Design: LalaCreative
Photography: Harper Point Photography

Printed in the United States of America.
10 9 8 7 6 5 4 3 2 1

ISBN-13: 978-1-7328916-0-9 (hardcover)
ISBN-13: 978-1-7328916-1-6 (softcover)

# Blessing

अन्नपूर्णे सादापूर्णे शङ्करप्राणवल्लभे ।
ज्ञानवैराग्यसिद्ध्यर्थं भिक्षां देहि च पार्वती ॥

*Annapoorne Sada Poorne*
*Shankara Prana Vallabhe*
*Jnana Vairagya Sidhyartham*
*Bhiksham Dehi Cha Parvati*

Annapurna, mother earth goddess of nourishment and
abundance (prakriti), I humbly ask for food to nourish my
body always. For the nourishment of my mind, give me
knowledge and wisdom to free my spirit. For the nourishment
of my spirit, remove my ignorance (avidya) and infatuation
with material attachments that keep me from being free.

*I dedicate this book to Anandmayee Maa, my spiritual guide.*
*My gift for you ~ Bina Mehta*

# Contents

Foreword i

Preface iii

About Ayurveda: "Knowledge of Life" v

About the Author ix

Introduction 2

   Spices: The Soul of Indian Cuisine 3

   Tempering: Unlocking the Essence of Spices 5

   Ghee: A Healthy Fat 10

   Dahls and Rice: Healthy and Familiar 11

   Sprouting: Creating Living Superfoods 11

   Fermenting: Balancing the Gut 13

   Paneer: A Special Treat 14

   Indian Breads: More Than Just Naan 16

   Deep-Frying: A Smart Indulgence 16

   Stock Up on Kitchen Equipment 19

   Get Your Pantry Ready 20

Chapter 1: North Indian Menu 21

Chapter 2: Gujarati Menu 41

Chapter 3: Bombay Street Food 59

Chapter 4: South Indian Menu 75

Chapter 5: Ethnic Specialties 91

Chapter 6: Ayureveda Menu 111

Chapter 7: Light Dinner Menu 129

Chapter 8: Indian Breakfasts 147

Chapter 9: Party Menu 163

Chapter 10: 4th of July Indian Style 177

Chapter 11: Chutneys 195

Frequently Asked Questions 204

Glossary 210

Index 221

Acknowledgments 224

# Foreword

What a blessing to hold the recipes and wisdom of Bina Mehta, yoga teacher, Ayurvedic lifestyle counselor, artist, mother, entrepreneur, and lover of the healing power of delicious and nutritious Indian cooking—the way she was taught in her family lineage.

Food (ana) is life-force, and our body is our "food body" (anamayakosha), directly translating into how we feel, flow, and metabolize life. In Ayurvedic wisdom, healing through food involves balancing the healing properties of herbs, tastes, elements, seasons, our enjoyment of food, and our realization of the gift of life. In short, you are what you eat.

Bina's offering gives us her special recipes, many using spices from her amazing gourmet spice blends (available at binamehta.com). This cookbook, *Turmeric & Spice,* offers not only the delights of several regions of India but also delicious detoxifying food that supports digestive health. These healing foods can be incorporated whenever you are feeling your digestion or immune system is off—or if you just want a lighter meal.

Bina's devotion through her heart, voice, teachings, embodiment in yoga, and cooking are her great gifts that we celebrate and now benefit from directly.

May you enjoy these recipes as food for life.

*Shiva Rea, Global Yoga teacher and founder of Prana Vinyasa*

**Below is a beautiful blessing and prayer from Bina's homeland.**

| | |
|---|---|
| Anam Brahman Raso Vishnu | अन्नम ब्रह्मा रसो विष्णु |
| Pakto Devo Maheshvaraha | पक्तो देवो महेश्वरः |
| Evam Jnatva Tu-yo-bhunkte | एवं ज्ञात्वा तूयोभुंक्ते |
| Anadosho Na Lipyate | अन्नदोषो न लिप्यते |
| Yatha Pinde Tatha Brahmade | यथा पिंड तथा ब्रह्मदे |

Food is Consciousness.
The fluid in the body is the Protector.
The fire which digests the food is the Transformer.
If you know this, the food becomes pure consciousness.

As in the macrocosm, so in the microcosm.
As above, so below.

# Preface

## To Eat Is Human; to Digest Is Divine

Have you ever prepared the same recipe, without changing the ingredients or their amounts, and experienced different results than expected? If so, did you wonder why this happened?

Cooking is more than just mechanically following a recipe. Think of what you are really doing: You are transforming an assortment of individual ingredients, using methods that have an important flow, into a dish that explodes with flavor. The spirit you bring into the kitchen is part of that process as well. If you are impatient or uninspired or tired, the dish will reflect that.

Cooking is a sacred and artful process. It is a creative blending, assimilation, and presentation of tastes, textures, techniques, and ingredients, causing that explosion of flavor in your mouth. Through my journey with food and my love and passion for cooking, I discovered there was something beyond mastering these flavors and techniques. A new taste emerged from the six basic tastes—sweet, sour, salty, astringent, pungent, and bitter—that I call the seventh taste. Consider that the essence of the rose is its fragrance, the essence of the mango is its sweetness, and the essence of beholding a glorious sunset is its inexplicable beauty. We have all experienced these moments at some time or another. When it happens with food, it is so much more than delicious—there is an aura of the extraordinary in the ordinary. It is a harmonious and sensual tasting and relishing with the colors, aromas, sounds, and flavors coupled with mind and heart simultaneously. It is in line with a concept in India called rasa, and so I call this seventh taste rasa.

When we encounter rasa, we experience pure delight and bliss. Like hopes, dreams, emotions, and thoughts, rasa cannot be measured but can be felt and experienced. Three things happen: the body tastes it, the heart feels delight, and the mind goes into a sort of rapture. Relishing and savoring the essence of food is the "juiciness" that defines rasa. Subtle, but all-encompassing; there is no mistaking the feeling that naturally, spontaneously, and effortlessly arises from the communion of the five elements (earth, water, fire, air, and ether), the senses, mind, body, and spirit, which is called sahaja. This is a state of being that athletes refer to as being "in the zone."

Rasa comes from mindful cooking that transforms food using thoughtful techniques. Treating this process mindfully creates experiential memories that will guide you each time you encounter not only the same recipe, but also new ones; you will have all the tools you need to make it soar.

In *Turmeric & Spice: Indian Cuisine for the Mind, Body, and Spirit,* I have infused rasa and celebrate the artistry of authentic Indian cuisine. Whether you eat meat or are a vegetarian or are on a diet that's dairy-free or gluten-free, you'll discover just how wildly versatile Indian cuisine is. Authentic Indian cooking is pleasing to the palate, is appealing to the mind, and can improve your nutrition, digestion, and longevity.

I have also included aspects of Indian philosophy and ancient Ayurvedic wisdom designed for the healthy balance of mind, body, and spirit. According to Ayurveda, to eat is human; to digest is divine. These philosophical principles guide my approach to cooking.

The recipes are organized by regional and specialty menus. You can mix and match as you like, but they are presented so that you can see a typical authentic menu. Authentic Indian cooking requires a bit of preparation and timing, but you'll find the journey well worth it. Once you've mastered the processes, it's easy! Authentic Indian cooking requires a bit of preparation, timing, and practice. But as you become familiar, you will become confident, and soon you'll be creating magical dishes and maybe even your own recipes.

To help you create this cuisine, I have included guidance on:

- Cooking with spices, aromatics, and herbs
- Sourcing the freshest ingredients and utensils
- Methods of preparation
- Key techniques and processes
- Proportionate assembly
- Using judgment
- Timing

I wrote this book to help you cook authentic Indian cuisine, but more importantly, I want you to enjoy this creative journey, reaping the rewards and delighting in the experience that rasa can bring to your life! I have always expressed my love and caring to others through food. So come on this journey, and let me share my love of food with you.

Love
Bina

# About Ayurveda: "Knowledge of Life"

Ayurveda, considered an ancient medical science, originated in India 5,000 years ago. *Ayur* means "longevity" or "life," and *veda* refers to knowledge steeped in the ancient scriptures. It is a living science that changes from day to day and person to person. With today's focus on holistic health care, the philosophy of Ayurveda has gained tremendous popularity in the West as an alternative healing technique because of its holistic approach.

I was fortunate to have been raised with Ayurveda as a way of life. At the time, I took for granted the rich tradition I had received. Once I moved to the United States, I studied intensely and became aware of the significance of this way of life. I am thrilled to share the wisdom of Ayurveda through my cookbook, spice blends, and philosophy.

Ayurveda seeks optimal health by fully "digesting" experiences to balance life. This includes digesting all our life experiences, whether they be food, emotions, careers, or relationships. Remember "Goldilocks and the Three Bears"? Too much is excessive, too little is not enough, but the balance between the two is just right. Ayurveda will help you achieve the balance that is just right for you.

The philosophical principles of Ayurveda state that all aspects of the universe, including living beings, are composed of a unique combination of five elements—earth, water, fire, air, and ether. Different combinations of these five elements make up three doshas, or tridosha:

- **VATA** (ether and air elements) governs the movement of all voluntary and involuntary body functions, such as the nervous system, heartbeat, breathing, energy, and creativity.

- PITTA (fire and water) is responsible for metabolism, enzymes, hormones, digestion, pigmentation, body temperature, hunger, thirst, and courage.

- KAPHA (water and earth) helps with cohesion and lubrication of joints, the strength of the body, and patience.

Your unique biological blueprint or matrix (prakriti) is made up of these elements at the time of your conception. When all elements in your matrix are in balance, you have optimal health, mental clarity, and vitality. When your elements are imbalanced (vikruti), you are in dis-ease, and disease can set in.

At its core, Ayurveda strives to maintain balance within the body according to your unique dosha, which is a

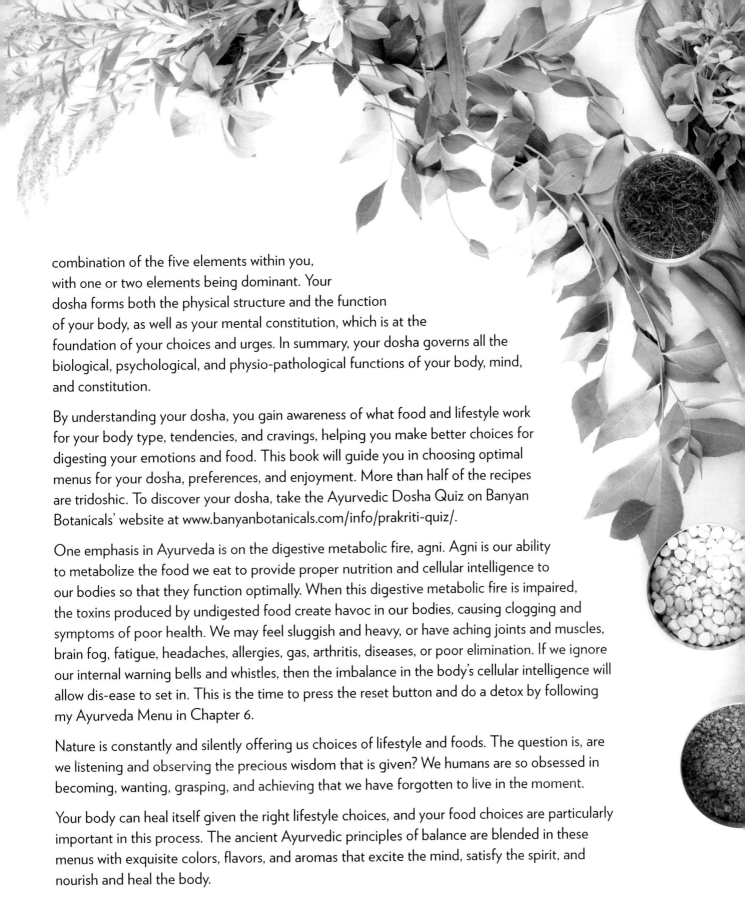

combination of the five elements within you, with one or two elements being dominant. Your dosha forms both the physical structure and the function of your body, as well as your mental constitution, which is at the foundation of your choices and urges. In summary, your dosha governs all the biological, psychological, and physio-pathological functions of your body, mind, and constitution.

By understanding your dosha, you gain awareness of what food and lifestyle work for your body type, tendencies, and cravings, helping you make better choices for digesting your emotions and food. This book will guide you in choosing optimal menus for your dosha, preferences, and enjoyment. More than half of the recipes are tridoshic. To discover your dosha, take the Ayurvedic Dosha Quiz on Banyan Botanicals' website at www.banyanbotanicals.com/info/prakriti-quiz/.

One emphasis in Ayurveda is on the digestive metabolic fire, agni. Agni is our ability to metabolize the food we eat to provide proper nutrition and cellular intelligence to our bodies so that they function optimally. When this digestive metabolic fire is impaired, the toxins produced by undigested food create havoc in our bodies, causing clogging and symptoms of poor health. We may feel sluggish and heavy, or have aching joints and muscles, brain fog, fatigue, headaches, allergies, gas, arthritis, diseases, or poor elimination. If we ignore our internal warning bells and whistles, then the imbalance in the body's cellular intelligence will allow dis-ease to set in. This is the time to press the reset button and do a detox by following my Ayurveda Menu in Chapter 6.

Nature is constantly and silently offering us choices of lifestyle and foods. The question is, are we listening and observing the precious wisdom that is given? We humans are so obsessed in becoming, wanting, grasping, and achieving that we have forgotten to live in the moment.

Your body can heal itself given the right lifestyle choices, and your food choices are particularly important in this process. The ancient Ayurvedic principles of balance are blended in these menus with exquisite colors, flavors, and aromas that excite the mind, satisfy the spirit, and nourish and heal the body.

# Understanding Your Unique Dosha

Fire  Water  Earth  Air  Ether

## VATA

When vata is unbalanced, too much uncertainty is accumulating in the mind, body, and spirit. As a result, you feel flighty and ungrounded. The best way to balance excess vata is to bring stability into your life.

- ○ Create a regular meditation and eating schedule.
- ○ Practice yoga to reconnect your mind with your body and environment.
- ○ Create a relaxing environment with fragrances, food, and music.
- ○ Eat foods that favor sweet, sour, and salty tastes.
- ○ Drink healing and relaxing herbal teas and warm soups.
- ○ Attempt to finish things once you have started them.

**The seasons of fall and early winter are the most important times to pacify vata.**

## PITTA

When pitta is unbalanced, too much frustration and anger are built up in the mind, body, and spirit. As a result, you feel internal and external combustion. The best way to balance excess pitta is to bring calmness into your life.

- ○ Eat in regular intervals to prevent hunger and anxiety.
- ○ Meditate regularly to soothe the mind and relax the body.
- ○ Create a relaxing environment or take a walk in nature and walk in the grass in bare feet.
- ○ Eat foods that favor sweet, bitter, and astringent tastes.
- ○ Drink healing and soothing herbal teas.
- ○ Engage in noncompetitive activities and be more playful.

**The seasons of late spring and summer are the most sensitive times of the year for pitta.**

## KAPHA

When kapha is unbalanced, too much depression is accumulating in the mind, body, and spirit. As a result, you feel fatigued and unmotivated. The best way to balance excess kapha is to bring joy and ignite motivation, intention, and action in your life.

- ○ Create opportunities for healthy activities and exercise.
- ○ Meditate regularly to determine your intentions and desires.
- ○ Create a colorful environment free of clutter and negativity.
- ○ Avoid overeating when you are not hungry and feeling emotional.
- ○ Eat foods that favor bitter, astringent, and pungent tastes.
- ○ Drink invigorating herbal teas.

**The seasons of late winter and spring are the best times to temper your kapha.**

# About the Author

*"Good health begins with the food we eat every day. Using the ancient principles of Ayurveda, not only can we eat delicious Indian food, but also we can promote healing of mind, body, and soul. Digestion of everything in our lives is the key."*

~Bina Mehta

Bina Mehta was raised in an Ayurvedic family in the exuberant city of Mumbai, India. Since moving to the United States, she has loved sharing the Indian culture with its respect for and adoration of food and vibrant living. Her knowledge of Indian cooking and her expertise on Ayurveda philosophy infuse her cookbook, *Turmeric & Spice*—in which she shares the wisdom she inherited from these ancient traditions—and her line of spice blends.

Immersed in the holistic field for more than 40 years, Bina has always had one goal: to draw out her clients' true, authentic potential. She is a certified Ayurvedic Lifestyle Consultant and was an assistant teacher in Contemplative Hinduism at the Naropa Institute in Boulder, Colorado. Bina has studied with many experts in their fields, including world-famous yogini Shiva Rea; Silvia Nakkach, yoga of voice instructor; and Ayurveda authority Vasant Lad and his protégé, Maria Garre.

In addition, Bina has explored many alternative healing modalities. She is a certified Universal White Time Healing instructor and assistant teacher, and has been studying with Fort Collins-based spiritual teacher Zari Pirasteh since 2004. Bina sees clients at her Fort Collins and Denver offices weekly, as well as offers distance healings and classes upon request.

All of Bina's passions form a congruent flow of healing knowledge that she combines to help people in many different facets of their lives.

# Bina Mehta Spice Blends

When Bina's cooking class students asked for pre-blended spices they could use at home with ease, she got to work developing a line of gourmet spice blends. She drew inspiration from formal Ayurveda study, family-rooted experiences, and insights gathered from teaching Indian cooking. The freshly roasted spices are uniquely blended for optimum aroma and maximum flavor.

The spice blends—recommended for beginners as well as culinary connoisseurs—elevate daily meals and are a time-saving treat for busy families and professionals. People who adore authentic Indian cuisine but don't wish to stock the multiple spices necessary to make them, can use the blends for making curries, lentils, and so much more.

Bina's blends include the six flavors identified in Ayurveda as necessary to fully satisfy the palate, balance the five elements of Hindu philosophy (earth, water, fire, air, and ether), and maintain a strong digestive fire. According to Ayurveda, spices not only are a very effective way to get intense, bright flavors into your diet, but also have been shown to benefit digestion and the immune system.

Bina's gourmet spice blends include Bombay Masala, Chai Masala, Garam Masala, Maharani Masala, and Roasted Cumin. You can purchase them individually or in a set at binamehta.com.

# Introduction

Indian food is exquisite because of its spice-filled flavor, intense aroma, and beautiful presentation. Add to that the infusion of rasa, the "seventh taste" that triggers pure delight of both the senses and the spirit.

Sound impossible to re-create in your own kitchen? It is not. In this section, you will learn about the basic ingredients and methods in Indian cooking: spices, ghee, tempering, dahls and rices, sprouting, fermenting, paneer, breads, and deep-frying. Stocking your kitchen with the right equipment and staples rounds out this introduction.

Master these processes and the rasa will come.

A few details to note:

- All temperatures are in Fahrenheit and use English measures.
- In all recipes calling for vegetables and herbs, it's best to have them washed, chopped, and ready before starting.

# Spices: The Soul of Indian Cuisine

Originally used as preservatives and medicines, spices are essential ingredients in every Indian kitchen and part of the whole culinary experience. The East has transformed the palate of the West with spices.

Masala is defined as a mixture of ground spices used in Indian cooking. While there is no rule of thumb for spice combinations, certain masala blends have different names and different uses. For example, garam masala is usually a combination of cinnamon, nutmeg, cloves, cardamom, mace, peppercorns, coriander, and cumin, and is found in many dishes. Some recipes in this book call for a specific masala, while others call for specific spices without a masala name. Once you've learned the properties of masala and gained experience—which ingredients to use, when, and how much—you can be adventurous and create your own blends.

In an Indian kitchen, you will have at your fingertips nature's pharmacy because spices have powerful healing qualities. They boost your immune system, detoxify organs and tissues, and optimize your metabolism. Our body heals itself when it is in balance, and the healthy properties in spices help bring the balance that the body needs to do this work.

Recipes for Indian cuisine can include the following: amchur powder, bay leaves, black pepper, cardamom (whole green pods), cinnamon (sticks and powder), cloves (whole and ground), coriander seeds, cumin (seeds and ground), curry leaves, fennel seeds, fenugreek seeds, garam masala, hing, mustard seeds, paprika, poppy seeds, rasam powder, red chili powder, saffron, salt, sambhar powder, tamarind paste, or turmeric. If you're not quite ready for a full spice cupboard like this, you can start by using my spice blends (binamehta.com). Substitutions of my spice blends are noted with individual recipes.

Turmeric in particular, a frequent ingredient in Indian dishes, is a power spice. Turmeric has gained immense popularity for its healing properties and disease prevention, and has helped chronic and debilitating diseases with no adverse effects. It contains a compound called curcumin, which is what helps fight and reverse diseases by bringing cellular intelligence in the body.

One note: Westerners coined the term *curry* to mean a single, all-purpose powder found in the grocery store. These powders can have different combinations of spice ingredients. But in fact, curry is the name of a dish that can have any unique combination of spices, herbs, aromatics, and seasonings.

You might want to invest in a masala dabba, a stainless steel round box that contains six to eight mini-containers for storing the most commonly used spices for cooking. Every Indian cook owns this. I call it "the spice garage." Not only does it look beautiful with the various colored spices, but it also makes spices readily available for cooking with ease and speed.

## To roast or not to roast?

Roasting spices, which can be done on the stovetop or in the oven, extracts the natural robust flavors and releases the essence and aromatic oils. The wafting aromatics whet your appetite, and health benefits are released. Dry-roasting spices provides an explosion of additional flavor and aromas that can transform your dish from delicious to amazing! While roasting takes a bit of effort, roasted spices last for years if prepared and stored properly.

Tips for roasting spices:

- Use whole spices. When I dry-roast spices, I am roasting seeds that are whole and raw—for example, whole cardamom, cumin, cloves, dried chilies, coriander, and cinnamon.

- Go slow. It is easy to slow-roast spices, but timing is important. If spices are overcooked, they will taste bitter.

- Roast in bulk. When you find a roasted spice recipe that you love, you can double or triple the batch. I always make large batches so that I can make my recipes quickly by eliminating the roasting step.

- Stovetop roasting: Heat a heavy-bottomed skillet to medium-high. Put your spices into the hot pan and shake the pan constantly, so they don't stick or burn. When they become fragrant and start to darken, they are sufficiently roasted and should be tipped out of the pan and cooled before grinding.

- Oven roasting: Place the spices in an 8x10-inch metal baking pan and roast at 350 degrees for 10 minutes until their aromas are released. Remove from the oven and transfer to a bowl to prevent overcooking. Once cool, they can be ground with a mortar and pestle or a coffee grinder.

- Store the roasted spices in a sterilized glass container with a lid to prevent excess moisture buildup and loss of flavor and aroma. It is disheartening to see your favorite expensive spice blend ruined!

### Whole Spice Conversions

Whole spices store better than ground spices, which lose flavor, especially if they are not roasted. If you don't want to roast spices, stock whole ones. The following chart shows how much of a whole spice makes a ground spice.

**Black pepper:** 1 teaspoon peppercorns = 1 ½ teaspoons ground

**Cardamom:** Approximately 12 pods, husked = 1 teaspoon ground

**Cinnamon:** One 1 ½-inch stick = 1 teaspoon ground

**Coriander:** 1 teaspoon coriander seeds = 1 ¼ teaspoons ground

**Cumin:** 1 teaspoon cumin seeds = 1 ¼ teaspoons ground

**Fennel:** 1 teaspoon fennel seeds = 1 ¼ teaspoons ground

**Mustard seeds:** 1 teaspoon mustard seeds = 1 ½ teaspoons ground

**Nutmeg:** ½ nutmeg = 1 teaspoon ground

## Tempering: Unlocking the Essence of Spices

Tempering—tadka or tarka—is at the heart of Indian cooking. Whole spices, seeds, herbs, and aromatics are added to hot oil or ghee, which are then added to a dish. This method produces the pleasing snap-crackle-pop sounds common in every Indian household, along with the wonderful aromas that linger in the air. It's no wonder that when friends enter our house, they say it smells so good!

In India—a country with regional, seasonal, cultural, and religious diversity—people unanimously agree that tempering transforms ordinary food into something extraordinary.

In northern India, it is called chaunkh; in western India, the Gujaratis call it vaghaar or baghaar; and in the south, it is called oggaranes. The method is found in other cultures' cuisines as well. Asians call it "stir-frying," and the French call it "sautéing." I have watched my Italian friend Phyllis finish her minestrone soup with garlic in fresh basil butter to enhance the flavors and bring balance to the dish.

The tempering process encapsulates two key concepts: heat and balance. Heating the spices releases their subtle essences and brings out their hidden flavors, aromas, and nutrients, as well as their aesthetic and healing qualities—all of which unite to permeate the entire dish.

Tempering is done with your choice of ghee or cooking oil. Use oils with a high smoke point for tempering, as it requires cooking over very high temperatures. Some oils can overheat and produce smoke. For example, olive oil has a low smoke point, so it isn't recommended for tempering. (See Deep-Frying on page 16 for a more detailed explanation of smoke points.) I like to use ghee, vegetable oil, safflower oil, or sunflower oil, though I prefer ghee since it renders the food flavorful.

Tempering can be done at the beginning or end of the cooking process. I typically do my tempering for rice pilaf in the beginning, adding cumin seeds, whole cinnamon sticks, cardamom pods, and bay leaves to the saucepan first. When the seeds are popping, I add the uncooked rice and blend it with the oil. Then I add water and season the mixture with saffron and salt and mix well. Stirring the rice while it cooks isn't recommended because it breaks the grains. For vegetables, I also temper in the beginning. The process is easy, but it requires preparation, judgment, and timing.

If you are making a dish with liquid ingredients—such as dahl, sambhar, khitchdi, or raita—it is best to temper at the end. Although there is no hard-and-fast rule, if you're boiling ingredients, you could lose the essence of your tempered ingredients if you temper them first. Use a separate saucepan when tempering at the end of a dish.

Typically, I prefer not to temper fresh herbs such as cilantro and mint since they are delicate. I use them at the end for a final finish and garnish.

**Things to remember:**

- Before starting the tempering process, have all the ingredients ready. You will be adding them in rapid succession, so you don't want to be fumbling with spice bottles and you don't want to burn the spices. The dish to be tempered should be ready, too. This process takes seconds to finish, so be prepared to move quickly once you begin.

- Heat your ghee or oil in a small saucepan on high, but do not allow the oil to smoke. One or two tablespoons of ghee is plenty for tempering. Once the oil is hot, reduce the heat to medium and start adding whole spices quickly, in rapid succession, until they splutter and crackle, or until mildly fragrant.

- The order in which you add ingredients is important. The whole seeds go first, and after they pop, add sliced pieces of ginger, sliced serranos, and curry leaves. If adding dry spices, take the pan off the stove to prevent them from burning.

- Tempering changes the color of the spices to a golden brown, and a powerful aroma is released. Be careful not to let them burn; timing is crucial because this can happen within seconds. If the ingredients are burnt, your nose will definitely tell you so. If this happens, start over—you don't want to ruin your dish with burned spices.

- Drizzle the tempered mixture on your dish as a final finish, and enjoy right away! This mixture must be used immediately and cannot be stored for use later.

These are some of the ingredients that can be tempered—but note that they would almost never all be used in the same dish.

- Bay leaves
- Cardamom (whole)
- Cinnamon sticks
- Cloves
- Cumin seeds
- Curry leaves

- Garlic
- Hing
- Mustard seeds
- Onion
- Red chilies

Once mastered, tempering is quick and easy and well worth it. You will enjoy a well-balanced symphony of flavors on your palate.

> Mystically, we temper to unlock the very unique essence that is within us. We temper, or bring into balance, all our vices and virtues by experiencing and learning from life's challenges by strengthening, purifying, refining, and distilling our true authentic self by living life to the fullest.

# Ghee: A Healthy Fat

Known as "liquid gold" and "golden nectar," ghee helps stimulate digestion. In Ayurvedic terms, it ignites agni, the fire in the belly that helps digest the food. According to Ayurveda, ghee is the most beneficial of all fats, is considered dairy-free, and enhances the flavor of food. It nourishes and lubricates internal organs and joints; dissolves toxins; alleviates fevers, anemia, and blood disorders; and promotes good health and well-being. One of the most stable fats, ghee reduces levels of LDL (bad) cholesterol and increases HDL (good) cholesterol, helps memory retention, and helps in detoxification.

Ghee is traditionally made by heating the unsalted butter made from cow or buffalo milk. Today, the best ghee is made from unsalted organic butter that comes from cows allowed to roam free and graze on green pastures. We call them happy cows.

The journey from milk to ghee starts with cream, which is collected from the milk for a few days. This is mixed and whipped and churned with soured yogurt until the whey separates and the solids become butter. The butter solids are then heated, which transforms the translucent, cloudy color into clear and transparent, revealing the beautiful golden color of ghee. It's no wonder it is called the most refined essence of milk; it's considered dairy-free at this stage.

An added bonus is that ghee has qualities of the five life force-giving elements: earth, water, fire, air, and ether. Ghee is called the superfood that balances all three doshas—vata, pitta, and kapha—and is especially good for balancing vata's frenzy and anxiety and calming and cooling the fiery pittas (see About Ayurveda on page v).

**Here is the recipe for making ghee:**

## Ghee
**Ingredient: 1 pound unsalted butter***

**Time: 15–20 minutes**

Melt the butter in a pot with a heavy bottom. Bring it to a boil over medium heat—do not cover. As it melts, the butter will separate into three layers. Do not stir. A clear foam will form on top, a golden liquid will float in the middle, and the milk solids will settle at the bottom.

Simmer the butter, which will produce a symphony of spluttering sounds and a nice aroma. As it cooks, white curds will appear on the surface, and the liquid will become cloudy. Reduce the temperature to medium-low and simmer again. Watch carefully to make sure the butter does not burn. Listen to the sound of the bubbles—the bubbles will dissipate as the moisture evaporates. After about 10 to 15 minutes, the bubbles will turn into a clear foam as the ghee is close to being done. At this time, you can use a clean, dry spoon to skim away the foam, revealing the clarified golden liquid, which is ghee.

Remove the pot from the stove and let cool to room temperature, allowing the solids to settle at the bottom. Then, carefully—leaving the solids undisturbed—strain the golden liquid through a cheesecloth and into a clean, dry glass jar. To avoid moisture buildup, make sure the liquid is completely cool before putting the lid on the jar. Store at room temperature for up to 1 month, or in the refrigerator indefinitely. One pound of unsalted butter makes 1 ½ cups of ghee.

*\* If you use more butter, it will take longer to cook.*

# Dahls and Rice: Healthy and Familiar

You will find many recipes in this book that call for different types of dahl and rice. Dahl is a daily staple in India. It is a generic name for a variety of pulses, which also includes lentils, dried peas, beans, and chickpeas. They are very high in protein and fiber and low in fat. Each type of dahl can come in three forms: whole, split with skin, or split and husked. Dahl varies from region to region in India; accordingly, recipes vary depending on the seasonal and regional varieties available. Dahls are served as main courses, soups, and side dishes, or used as a filling.

When cooking pulses, it is best to hold off adding salt or acids (such as lemon or vinegar) until the end, or else they will not soften or cook easily. Also, if your pulses are old, they will take longer to cook. For best results, soak and simmer pulses on low heat if you have the time. I've included cooking directions for the dahls in my recipes and in the chart on the next page.

In India, there are thousands of varieties of rice, but I use basmati and jasmine rice. I like a light, flavorful, fragrant long-grain rice. Rice is gluten-free and a versatile dish that can be eaten with dahl, vegetables, meat, and yogurt, and on its own. Rice is a star and staple of Southeast Asia.

# Sprouting: Creating Living Superfoods

Sprouting is a germinating process that transforms whole nuts, legumes, seeds, beans, grains, dried peas, and lentils into living superfoods. Living foods like sprouts are live at the time that we eat them and have their enzymes intact before cooking. The sprouting process enhances and enriches the nutritional quality of foods by elevating their levels of vitamins, minerals, fiber, and amino acids. It ignites the energy and life force in the bean or legume. Sprouts help with weight loss and lower blood cholesterol, purifying the blood and strengthening the immune system. Eating living foods vs. processed foods helps our bodies gain maximum benefit by bringing vitality, clarity, and radiance. That which is sprouted is alive.

Sprouting takes 2 to 3 days, so planning is necessary. This recipe is specifically sprouting whole mung beans and black chana, but the process is the same for sprouting whole beans, seeds, grains, legumes, and nuts. The weather and humidity will determine how quickly they sprout.

### Sprouting How-To

> **2 cups black chana** (makes 3 cups of sprouts)
> **2 cups mung beans** (makes 6 cups of sprouts)

Thoroughly wash and then soak 1 cup of mung beans in a large bowl with 8 cups of water for 8 to 10 hours. The beans will swell and double in size as the water is absorbed.

Drain the water completely using a colander.

Wrap the drained beans in a moist cheesecloth and place in a dry bowl. Put the bowl in a dark, well-ventilated place for 16 to 18 hours and allow the beans to germinate. Keep them moist—

every 8 hours, rinse the cheesecloth, drain well, and place in a dry bowl to continue germinating. You will see tiny shoots emerging from the beans.

Continue sprouting until the sprouts are about ½ to 1 inch long. Remove them from the cheesecloth and store in sealed plastic bags or containers in the refrigerator. Use within 3 to 4 days.

Eat them raw in my awesome Sprouted Mung Salad (recipe on page 136), use them in place of mung dahl in Khitchdi (recipe on page 114), or stir-fry them with spices and enjoy on rice with yogurt.

## Dahl and Rice Chart

| | Description | Soak | Cook Time (simmer) | Sample Recipe | Notes |
|---|---|---|---|---|---|
| Massoor Dahl | Red, orange, or pink lentils | 2 hours | 45 minutes | Massoor Dahl and Spinach (page 140) | |
| Toovar Dahl | Beige or yellow lentils, sometimes called split pigeon peas; an Indian staple | 6 hours | 1 hour 20 minutes on medium, covered | Sambhar (page 86) | |
| Whole Mung | Green whole beans | 6-8 hours | 1 hour 20 minutes on medium-high, covered; if sprouted, 5 minutes | Sprouted Mung Salad and Dressing (page 136) Pani Puri (page 65) | Can be sprouted; cook time = 10 minutes after sprouted |
| Mung Dahl/ Split Mung Dahl | Petite yellow lentils; split, these are dehusked mung beans | 2 hours | 20 minutes on medium-high | Mung Dahl and Spinach (page 45) Mung Dahl Bhajias (page 174) | |
| Urad Dahl (whole) | Black gram lentils, split and dehusked | 6 hours | 1 hour 20 minutes on medium-high, covered | Maa Ki Dahl (page 27) | |
| Urad Dahl (split or dehusked) | Black on the outside, white inside | 3-4 hours | 45 minutes on medium, covered | Traditional Dosa (page 78) and Idli (page 82) | |
| Chickpeas | Known as garbanzo beans in the U.S., and beige or yellow in color; called chole when cooked | 6-8 hours | 30 minutes on medium, covered | Chole (page 161) | If sprouted, 1 hour |
| Kala Chana | Small black garbanzo beans (chickpeas) | 6-8 hours | 1 hour 5 minutes on medium, covered | Black Chana Salad (page 155), Pani Puri (page 65), Vitamin Bhel Salad (page 158) | If sprouted, 20 minutes |
| Chana Dahl | Split black chana | 2 hours | 30 minutes on medium, covered | Trevti Dahl (page 128) Maa Ki Dahl (page 27) | |
| Rajma | Red kidney beans | 6-8 hours | 1 hour 30 minutes on medium, covered | Rajma Dahl (page 175) | |
| Besan | Garbanzo bean (chickpea) flour, yellow or cream in color | No | 20 minutes on medium, covered | Pakora (page 57) Vadaa Paav (page 68) | Use as a gluten-free thickening agent |
| Basmati Rice | White long-grain rice from India | No | 15 minutes on high, 5 minutes covered | Fragrant Saffron Basmati Rice (page 137), Biryani Rice (page 96), Caramelized Rice (page 106) | |

## Fermenting: Balancing the Gut

Hippocrates said you are only as healthy as your digestion and all diseases begin in the gut. Equilibrium in our gut flora—our beneficial bacteria—is essential for mental, emotional, and spiritual health. Poor digestive fire (agni) causes toxins (ama) resulting in dis-ease or disease. As your gut flora becomes more balanced, the functioning of your brain improves as does your mood.

Fermented foods are living foods and probiotic powerhouses. Consuming fermented foods rebuilds the flora in the digestive track, aids in weight loss, and detoxifies the body. By introducing fermented foods in your diet, you will repopulate and reseed the gut to rebuild and regenerate the integrity of the stomach lining naturally. Our ancestors used fermented foods to increase nutritional value and preserve foods before refrigerators existed. Fermented foods are common in Indian cuisine, and even today, people take fermented foods on long journeys because they don't spoil easily.

Fermentation is a natural process by which complex substances are predigested into simple substances. Fermented foods are living foods that enhance the nutrition we derive from the food and reduces the energy required by the body to digest, assimilate, and absorb nutrition easily and quickly.

A number of recipes in this book call for fermenting lentils or grains, both of which require planning ahead. It takes time to soak, grind, and allow the batter to rise, but the result is well worth the wait. Temperature and humidity can affect the fermentation or rising process. The warmth of summer speeds it up; the cool temperatures of winter inhibit the activity of culture growth, requiring more time. Cold temperatures can make the process take 18 to 24 hours, while the same results in summer are produced in 9 to 15 hours. You're looking for little bubbles to form and for the mixture to increase by one-third of its original size. The fermented batter can be stored in a sealed container in the refrigerator for up to 10 days.

I hope you enjoy and quickly feel the benefits of adding living foods, such as dosas, idlis, mung dahl bhajias, and yogurt to your diet. Each of these has its own process, which is explained in the recipe.

## Paneer: A Special Treat

Paneer is homemade Indian cheese made with cow's milk. This cheese has been made for over 6,000 years and is used as a base for cheesecakes, dips, sweets, and vegetable dishes. I was raised as a vegetarian in Mumbai, and Paneer Mutter (recipe on page 33) was one of my favorite dishes—I loved the taste, the texture, and the freshness of it.

Paneer has several extraordinary health benefits and is a fabulous source of protein and calcium, making it great for vegetarian diets. It protects against heart disease by lowering the fat deposition in arteries. As an inherent source of conjugated linoleic acid, an essential fatty acid, it fights cancer, helps with weight loss, and limits food allergy reactions. Eat paneer to prevent chronic illness.

Paneer (recipe on page 36) is made by boiling milk and adding something acidic like vinegar. The milk is separated into curds and whey by straining the excess liquid (the whey) from the curds using a cheesecloth hung on the kitchen faucet for a few hours. The whey is full of good minerals and can be kept and used as a vegetarian broth. Squeeze and shape the paneer before refrigerating for 4 to 6 hours. Soak in a bath of salt water for a few minutes to create a gorgeous layer of sheen. This makes the cheese easier to cut and helps it hold its shape when added to dishes.

## Indian Breads—More Than Just Naan

In India, man can live on bread alone. The poor villagers who work in the fields pack a lunch that consists of one piece of bread (a kind of roti), one slice of onion, and one pickle. Before the British brought silverware to India, meals were eaten using pieces of bread that were broken off and dipped in dahl and then a vegetable. At home, it is still common to eat this way when there are no guests.

Though it is the one most familiar to Americans, Indian bread does not begin and end with naan. In fact, there are at least 40 varieties of Indian breads, differing from region to region and using their own flours and cooking techniques. Most are made with wheat flour, rice flour, millet flour (such as bajri, juwar, and ragi), corn flour, and multigrain flour. Indian breads range from flatbreads to crepes, and can be leavened or unleavened, baked, roasted, steamed, or fried—many are even gluten-free.

Wheat is grown primarily in northern India, and rice is grown primarily in the south, and the options available reflect this. In the north, you'll find more parathas, rotis, kachoris, puris, kulchas, bhatooras, and naans. Thalipeeth, satpadi, puran poli, bhakri, pudas, theplas, debras, rotlas, and pankis are found in India's midwest. In the south, there are several preparations of rice-based crepes: dosas, appams, and uthappams. The simplest type of bread is roti, which is eaten in both the north and south. It is commonly served at every meal. But there is no hard-and-fast rule regarding which type of bread must be served with which dish. The breads are very versatile.

All are an important part of Indian cuisine, used as scoops that allow us to soak up every bit of the delicious gravies, vegetables, and sauces, letting us lick our platters clean.

In this cookbook, you'll find recipes for parathas, puris, rotis, and naan. Experiment and enjoy!

## Deep-Frying: A Smart Indulgence

Love fried foods? Want to stay healthy? Get the best of both worlds! Don't believe the myth that deep-fried foods are bad for you. The benefits of healthy fats are innumerable. When healthy saturated fats are digested, they're broken down into fatty acids that convert food to energy that supports brain function, regulates insulin and the hormonal system, nourishes the immune system and nerve tissue, maintains the integrity and flexibility of our organs, and provides optimal joint lubrication and cell membrane protection.

Balance is the key. Ayurveda teaches us to not overdo it. If you eat deep-fried foods one day, balance it the next day with healthy greens. You are always feeding your mind and spirit while nourishing your physical body. Although Ayurveda does not forbid or deny anything, it also says "everything in moderation." To indulge is human, but to balance with moderation is divine.

Even if you're on an Ayurvedic diet, every now and then you can enjoy a tasty, crunchy, luscious deep-fried treat—a simple luxury that no one should be denied. (Try Mung Dahl Bhajias, page 174, or Vadaa Paav, page 68.) Fried foods are a delight, especially in fall and winter because they warm your palate and provide that essential crunch in every bite.

## How to Deep-Fry

Deep-frying isn't difficult; however, it does require knowing a few tips and having the right tools to make the process easy, fun, and successful. The two most important things you need to do are choose the right oil and fry the food at the correct temperature.

You'll need the following items:

- Dutch oven
- Dutch oven thermometer
- Metal spider skimmer or slotted spoon
- Paper towels

A Dutch oven with a heavy bottom will suffice for frying foods safely. A Dutch oven thermometer is a useful gadget you can attach to the side of the Dutch oven for a more accurate temperature reading. Once you master the technique of deep-frying, you won't need a thermometer. Metal skimmers made of wire or stainless steel will help you retrieve the food and drain excess hot oil from a safe distance. Use paper towels to drain or pat excess oil from food before serving.

## The Right Temperature

In the deep-frying process, you submerge food in hot oil on medium to high heat while maintaining an ideal temperature of 350 to 375 degrees. Maintaining the correct oil temperature renders the food light and crunchy, instead of greasy and soggy. If the temperature drops below 300 degrees, the food saturates in oil and sinks to the bottom of the fryer. If it's too hot, the outer crust burns while the inside filling either burns too or remains uncooked. The correct temperature will form a beautiful, crunchy, golden-brown seal that locks in the natural moisture and juicy flavor of the food while protecting it from deep oil penetration.

## The Right Oil

Choosing the correct oil is critical because of the smoke point, the temperature at which the oil overheats, producing smoke and fumes that destroy many nutrients in unrefined oils and impart a burnt flavor to foods. This is also very detrimental to health, so make sure you use an oil with a high smoke point when deep-frying (as well as when grilling and pan-frying). This type of oil is stable for high temperature cooking.

Oils that are delicate and have a low smoke point are used for salad dressings and drizzling over food. Although olive oil is an excellent choice for many types of cooking, it's not recommended for deep-frying due to its low smoke point.

I cook a lot with homemade ghee (see page 10). I enjoy the glorious sizzle and the burst of bubbles as I add food to the hot oil.

Here are the smoke points of various oils, from highest to lowest. Feel free to choose the oil that you prefer:*

Avocado oil 520°F

Safflower oil 510°F

Rice bran oil 490°F

Ghee 485°F

Peanut oil 450°F

Sunflower oil 440°F

Sesame oil 410°F

Grapeseed oil 405°F

Coconut oil 400°F

Olive oil 375°–405°F (extra virgin), 390°F (virgin)

Butter 350°F

Flax oil 225°F

*Note: Reheating an oil lowers the smoke point of even the best oils. Using it once or twice on the same day, however, is acceptable.*

**Safety Tip**

Remember, hot oil and water are not friends, so while frying, dry your hands, instruments, and containers completely because splattering oil could be a hazard.

## Stock Up on Kitchen Equipment

If you cook, I imagine you have your own favorite utensils. These are the tools that I use regularly, but they can be substituted with what you already have in your kitchen arsenal.

- A sharp set of knives is absolutely essential for preparing vegetables and meats.

- A good coffee grinder is helpful for grinding roasted spices. I dedicate one grinder for spices, so their residue doesn't infiltrate my morning coffee.

- Ladles and stainless steel serving spoons for rice, lentils, and vegetables are all available at your favorite cookware store or at Indian grocery stores. They are versatile in any kitchen.

- 10-inch and 12-inch Circulon Infinite Skillets (twin pack) are great for making rotis, parathas, and scrambled eggs.

- A small stainless steel saucepan is very helpful for tempering ingredients.

- Stainless steel pans with a copper core conduct heat evenly. My cookware is durable, safe for the oven, and does not develop rust—I have had it for years. This no-maintenance, no-fuss cookware can be scraped and scrubbed with any cleaning material.

- A spider skimmer is a special frying tool used by many Asian cultures and is available in Asian markets. It is a metal basket with a long metal or bamboo handle. It ranges in price from $2 to $30, but I see no reason, other than personal preference, to pay the higher prices. If you do any kind of frying in your kitchen, this tool is indispensable.

- A Dutch oven or kadhai is essential for deep-frying.

- I recommend a pressure cooker because it shortens the cooking time, which is helpful when you're in a hurry. With a pressure cooker, you can make a meal from start to finish within an hour.

- I also recommend adding a candy thermometer and cheesecloth to your kitchen toolbox.

# Get Your Pantry Ready

**STAPLES LIST**

### Refrigerator

Butter, unsalted (to make ghee)

Lemons

Limes

Milk, whole

Yogurt, plain

### Pantry

Chickpeas

Coconut milk

Dahl or pulses (lentils, dried peas, and beans; see Dahl Chart on page 12)

Flour (white, wheat, or besan)

Mung beans

Oil (see How to Deep-Fry on page 17)

Onions/green onions

Rice: jasmine, basmati, and long-grain white

Serrano chilies

Sugar

Tomatoes, canned

### Herbs and spices

Ajwain seeds

Amchur powder

Bay leaves

Black pepper; black peppercorns

Cardamom, whole or powder

Cilantro leaves

Cinnamon: powder or stick

Cloves

Coriander: powder, seeds

Cumin: powder (roasted), seeds*

Curry leaves

Curry paste, hot or mild

Fenugreek seeds

Garlic, whole or paste

Ginger, whole or powdered

Hing

Masala (garam, chaat, dabba, dhansak, paav bhaaji, bombay, maharani, chai)**

Mint leaves

Mustard seeds (black or yellow)

Rasam powder

Red chili powder

Saffron

Salt

Sambhar powder

Tamarind powder or sauce

Turmeric powder

*Or try Bina's Roasted Cumin spice blend (binamehta.com)*

**Or try Bina's Bombay Masala, Garam Masala, or Maharani Masala spice blends (binamehta.com)*

Aloo gobi, butter chicken, paneer spinach saag, tandoori chicken, kebabs, saffron rice, eggplant bharta, naan, roti, and dahl—these are the foods of the North Indian regions such as Punjab, Kashmir, Massoorie, Shimla, and Delhi, the capital. The northern climate is hardy, with extreme temperatures in both summer and winter. People eat chicken and lamb grilled or in cream sauces, and indigenous breads made in clay ovens called tandoors. This area is the granary of India—wheat is the predominant crop. "Let's go eat roti" is a colloquial saying that means "I am hungry. Let's go have lunch (or dinner)."

One experience in northern India is eating at dhabas, small outdoor food stalls commonly found on roadsides that serve fresh-cooked vegetables, naans, kebabs, chicken and lamb, rajma, rice, and chai. These are a mecca for food lovers because they're affordable and tasty and conveniently located on highways and major interstate routes. Travelers young and old, poor or rich, all stop at their favorite dhaba for a snack or a meal. It's a fun experience.

By savoring the food of the north, we experience the rich history of blended cultures. North India's exotic past is full of stories about the lavish lifestyles of the kings, queens, and their palaces in the Himalayas. Akbar, the Mughal king of the 16th century, promoted tolerance of other faiths. He set an example by marrying a princess from each faith and allowing the lifestyle and food of their choice in his palace. A multitude of settlers and conquerors—Persians, Mughals, British—brought a mélange of cultures and belief systems that now coexist. This kaleidoscope of variety is reflected in the food, which is very Hindu-Muslim dominant.

# Chapter 1

# North Indian Menu

Tandoori Chicken                    23

Chicken Tikka Masala                26

Maa Ki Dahl                         27

Saag                                29

Roasted Eggplant Bharta             32

Paneer Mutter                       33

Paneer                              36

Achari Aloo                         37

Bundi Raita                         38

Naan                                39

# *Tandoori Chicken*  तंदूरी मुर्ग

Tandoori Chicken is a North Indian favorite and a specialty of dhabas (roadside cafes). The chicken is marinated in yogurt and spices and traditionally cooked in a special clay oven called a tandoor. This is a spicy dish that is great for grilling. Tandoori Chicken is the base for Chicken Tikka Masala (recipe on page 26).

3 ½ pounds boneless, skinless chicken breasts and thighs

3 cups plain yogurt

3 tablespoons mustard oil (optional)

3 tablespoons lemon juice

1 tablespoon garlic paste

1 tablespoon ginger paste

1–2 serrano chilies, finely diced

3 tablespoons finely chopped cilantro leaves

3 tablespoons finely chopped mint leaves

1 tablespoon roasted cumin powder (or try Bina's Roasted Cumin)

2 tablespoons garam masala (or try Bina's Garam Masala)

4 tablespoons Patak's mild or hot curry paste (see page 205)

3 tablespoons tandoori masala powder

1 tablespoon salt (or to taste)

¼ teaspoon saffron (optional)

Wash the chicken thoroughly in cold water, pat dry, and score lightly in a few places.

Mix all the remaining ingredients in a bowl. Add the chicken to the marinade, and refrigerate for 8 to 14 hours until ready to grill. Save the leftover marinade for Chicken Tikka Masala, providing it's made on the same day.

Spray the grill with cooking oil, then preheat the grill on medium-high. Bring the marinated chicken to room temperature before grilling.

Shake off the excess marinade, then put the chicken on the grill. Grill for 10 to 15 minutes on each side, covered, until the juices run clear or a meat thermometer reads 155 degrees. Take it off the grill, and let it rest, covered, for 5 to 10 minutes to reach the finished temperature of 165 degrees. Serve and enjoy.

This basic recipe can be served as chicken kebabs or used in Chicken Tikka Masala.

**Serves 6 to 8.**

# Chicken Tikka Masala  मुर्ग टिक्का मसाला

Chicken Tikka Masala, or butter chicken, is Tandoori Chicken with a creamy sauce. You can make this delicious sauce while the chicken is on the grill. Enjoy!

4 tablespoons ghee

2 cups finely chopped onions

½ tablespoon minced garlic

4 tablespoons milk (substitute dairy-free milk if needed)

2 tablespoons sugar (optional)

¼ cup tomato paste (from 1 can)

1 tablespoon salt

4 cups grilled Tandoori Chicken, cut into 2-inch cubes

2 serrano chilies, finely minced (optional)

2 tablespoons tandoori masala powder, for color and extra flavor (optional)

2–3 tablespoons Patak's mild curry paste (see page 205)

4 tablespoons Tandoori Chicken marinade (saved from recipe on page 23)

½ teaspoon red chili powder

1 teaspoon garam masala (or try Bina's Garam Masala)

2 cups cream or coconut milk

2 tablespoons chopped cilantro leaves

Heat the ghee in a large skillet on medium-high until hot but not smoking. Add the onions and sauté for 8 to 10 minutes, or until translucent. Add the garlic and sauté for 2 minutes.

Stir the milk and sugar (if desired) into the skillet and heat for 30 seconds. Add the tomato paste, salt, grilled chicken cubes, serrano chilies (if desired), tandoori masala (if desired), curry paste, marinade, chili powder, and garam masala. Mix well and remove from the heat.

Just before serving, add the cream to the skillet and return to medium heat for 10 minutes, stirring constantly, until bubbles form. (If the heat is too high, the cream will curdle.)

Garnish with cilantro and serve.

**Serves 6 to 8.**

# Maa Ki Dahl (Black Dahl) मां की दाल

This dahl is a staple in every North Indian household. It's made with urad, rajma, and chana beans and can be simmered in a pot all day to meld flavors nicely. It's hearty and easy to make, and a great accompaniment with rice, roti, or naan. In restaurants, this recipe is typically loaded with butter and cream, but my recipe is a lighter version that tastes even better!

1 ¾ cups whole urad dahl (or black dahl; see Dahl Chart on page 12)

¼ cup rajma (kidney beans)

2 tablespoons chana dahl (split black chickpeas)

¼ teaspoon fenugreek seeds (methi), optional

8–10 cups water

2 tablespoons grated ginger

1 bay leaf

2 whole cardamom pods

2 tablespoons salt (or to taste)

3 tablespoons tomato paste

3 tablespoons ghee

2 cups chopped onions (about 2 medium onions)

1 serrano chili, sliced in half (optional)

1 tablespoon ground coriander

½ teaspoon roasted cumin powder (or try Bina's Roasted Cumin)

1 tablespoon garam masala (or try Bina's Garam Masala)

¼ teaspoon cinnamon powder

¼ teaspoon ground cloves

Chopped cilantro leaves

1 tablespoon lime juice (or to taste)

In a large bowl, soak the urad dahl, rajma, chana dahl, and fenugreek (if desired) in the water overnight (10 to 15 hours). The lentils and beans will double in size.*

Pour the mixture into a large pot.** Add the ginger, bay leaf, cardamom, and salt. Bring to a boil, then reduce the heat to low, cover, and simmer for 1 hour 20 minutes. The beans are done when they are soft. Use a ladle or spoon to press some of the beans against the side of the pot while warm; mashing some of the mixture will give it a thick consistency. Add the tomato paste and mix.

While the beans are simmering, heat the ghee in a small skillet on medium-high. Once the skillet is hot, add the onions and serrano chili (if desired). Cook for 6 to 10 minutes, or until the onions are translucent but not brown. Add the coriander, cumin, garam masala, cinnamon, and cloves and mix well. Set aside.

When the beans are done, stir the onion mixture into the beans. Add water to desired consistency, if needed. Simmer for another 20 minutes. Before serving, remove the bay leaf and cardamom pods.

Garnish with cilantro and squeeze lime juice on top of each serving for added flavor.

Serve with Fragrant Saffron Basmati Rice (recipe on page 137), Naan (recipe on page 39), Parathas Stuffed with Radishes (recipe on page 150), or Chapattis (recipe on page 168)

**Serves 8.**

**\*Water:** This recipe tends to turn out well if you begin with the 8 cups of water to soak and add water as needed. The finished thickness is up to your general preference, but while simmering on the stove, the general rule of covering solids with 2 inches of water is helpful. Some water will evaporate or become absorbed, and you want to have enough water in your pot to avoid burning. Be sure to stir often to keep the bottom from sticking, and add water throughout to maintain a proper level.

**\*\*Pressure cooker option:** Place the beans, water, ginger, bay leaf, cardamom, and salt in a pressure cooker and close the lid. When the pressure cooker starts to whistle, continue cooking following your cooker's directions. Do not force the cooker to open; wait until the pressure subsides. Once the pressure cooker settles and allows opening, use a ladle or the back of a spoon to crush some of the beans to thicken the dahl. Discard the bay leaf and cardamom pod. Continue the recipe where the ghee directions begin.

# Saag (Spinach) साग

Eat more greens every day! Leafy, mild, and bitter greens are loaded with nutrition and low in calories. These are action-packed with the light and life force of the sun (chlorophyll) to help you feel more vibrant and energized. Add paneer or your favorite protein to enhance the dish. Tip: The pinch of baking soda keeps the greens green—but more than a pinch will ruin the taste!

½ cup ghee or oil of your choice

2 tablespoons sesame oil

4 cups finely diced onions

1 ½ tablespoons minced garlic

2 tablespoons grated ginger

1 can (16 ounces) crushed tomatoes

3 tablespoons Patak's mild curry paste (see page 205)

1 tablespoon salt

1 teaspoon turmeric powder

1 teaspoon cardamom powder

1 teaspoon garam masala (or try Bina's Garam Masala)

1 ½ tablespoons sugar (optional)

2 pounds baby spinach, frozen or washed if fresh, or a combination of your favorite fresh or frozen greens

3 tablespoons finely chopped mint leaves

3 tablespoons finely chopped cilantro leaves

2 serrano chilies, finely diced

Pinch of baking soda

Heat the ghee and sesame oil in a large skillet on medium-high. Add the onions and cook for 10 minutes, or until translucent but not brown, stirring constantly. Add the garlic and ginger, and cook for about 3 minutes. Turn up the heat to high and add the tomatoes and cook for 5 to 7 minutes, or until they break down. Mix in the curry paste.

Stir in the salt, turmeric, cardamom powder, garam masala, and sugar (if desired). Add the spinach, mint, cilantro, and serrano chilies. Sprinkle in the baking soda to keep the vegetables green. Simmer for about 20 minutes.

Using an immersion blender or in a food processor, blend the hot mixture to a smooth paste. Serve hot.

**Serves 6 to 8.**

# Roasted Eggplant Bharta भुना बैंगन भर्ता

To lose weight, eat more eggplant. There are only 20 calories in a cup of plain, roasted, mashed eggplant. It's tasty, too. Those who once cringed at the thought of eggplant have said this dish is amazing and are hooked on it.

2 large eggplants (see tips for choosing eggplant on page 214)

⅓ cup vegetable oil

2 cups chopped onions

1 tablespoon grated ginger

1 can (12 ounces) crushed tomatoes

½ cup chopped red bell peppers

1 cup chopped green bell peppers, or 1 cup peas

1 tablespoon fennel seeds

1 tablespoon ground coriander

1 tablespoon roasted cumin powder (or try Bina's Roasted Cumin)

½ teaspoon red chili powder

½ tablespoon salt (or to taste)

1 teaspoon turmeric powder

Cilantro leaves

Preheat the oven to broil. Poke each eggplant about four times with a large knife so that they do not burst while roasting. Place the whole eggplants on a cookie sheet in the middle rack of the oven and roast for 20 to 25 minutes, or until soft. Turn the eggplants every 10 minutes. For a smokier flavor, fire-roast on the grill.

Remove from the oven and make a slit in the center of the eggplants. Scoop the pulp out (like a baked potato), and discard the skin. Be mindful of the steam, and do not burn your hands. Mash the eggplant pulp with a spoon or potato masher while still warm.

Heat the oil in a medium skillet on medium-high. Sauté the onions and ginger for 3 minutes, or until translucent. Add the tomatoes and bell peppers until a gravy consistency is formed. Mix in the mashed eggplant.

Add the fennel seeds, coriander, cumin, red chili powder, salt, and turmeric to the mixture. Mix well and heat through.

Garnish with cilantro and serve hot.

**Serves 6 to 8.**

# Paneer Mutter (Cheese and Peas) पनीर मटर

Made with soft cheese and peas in a spiced tomato gravy, this is a simple, flavorful, popular dish that even children love. Serve it with naan or rice, or savor every bite on its own. For convenience, you can buy paneer at Indian grocery stores. You can make your own whey with store-bought paneer by soaking it in hot water for 2 hours.

1 pound Paneer (recipe on page 36)

2 cups whey

2 tablespoons vegetable oil

2 tablespoons ghee

2 cups diced onions

1 tablespoon grated ginger

1 can (16 ounces) crushed or diced tomatoes

1/2 cup water

1 1/2 cups frozen peas

1 tablespoon coriander seeds

1 tablespoon cumin seeds

1 1/2 tablespoons poppy seeds (white or black)

1/2 teaspoon red chili powder

1 tablespoon garam masala (or try Bina's Gourmet Garam Masala Spice Blend)

1 teaspoon turmeric powder

1/2 tablespoon salt

1/2 teaspoon sugar

2 tablespoons tomato paste

If the paneer is store-bought: Soak it in 2 cups hot water for 2 hours to make whey. Drain, reserving all the liquid. Cut the paneer into 1-inch cubes and set aside along with the whey.

If the paneer is homemade: No need to soak it. Cut it into 1-inch cubes and set aside along with the whey.

Heat a large skillet on medium-high, then add oil and ghee, and heat for about 30 seconds. Sauté the onions and ginger for 6 to 9 minutes, or until the onions are translucent. Add the tomatoes and cook on medium heat until they break down and the oil separates (called deglazing).

Put the mixture into a food processor or use an immersion blender to make a smooth sauce. Once blended, return it to the skillet. Add the water and peas, and simmer for 5 minutes, or until it bubbles.

In a small saucepan over medium-high heat, place the coriander seeds, cumin seeds, and poppy seeds and lightly roast for 4 minutes, or until fragrant. Allow the seeds to come to room temperature. Grind the seeds into a powder using a coffee grinder. If you don't want to grind your own seeds, use the Whole Spice Conversion's chart on page 5.

Stir the spices into the mixture in the skillet. Add the red chili powder, garam masala, turmeric, salt, and sugar and stir. Add the tomato paste and then the 2 cups whey.

Just before serving, add the paneer cubes to the skillet, and simmer until hot. For a thinner consistency, add 1/2 cup water.

Serve with rice or naan.

**Serves 6 to 8.**

*If you want your paneer to have a bright sheen, soak the block of paneer for 5 minutes in a bath of water with 1 tablespoon of salt added. Then drain and cut into cubes or store in the refrigerator.

# Paneer (Indian Fresh Cheese) पनीर

I grew up in a home where fresh paneer was not part of our vegetarian Gujarati diet, so for me, it was a special treat. I impatiently had to wait to eat this when our family would go out for dinner, which was not too often. My sister, even to this day, only orders paneer in a restaurant, and you can ask her how much we enjoy teasing her about it. Homemade is always better, but if you do not want to make this, it's available in the refrigerated section of all Indian grocery stores.

½ gallon whole milk

⅜ cup white vinegar

½ teaspoon salt

In a large pot with a heavy bottom, heat the milk on medium-high until it reaches 130 degrees on a candy thermometer. (It will be lukewarm to the touch.) Add the vinegar and salt. Stir the milk and vinegar in a figure eight with a wooden spoon. Continue stirring until the milk separates into curds (solids) and whey (liquid).

After it separates, turn off the heat, and take the pot off the stove.

Line a colander with cheesecloth so that it overlaps on the sides. If you choose to save the whey that is drained off in the next step, then put a pan under the colander to catch the whey. Otherwise, it can be discarded.

Pour the mixture into the colander to drain off the whey, leaving the curds in the cheesecloth. Gently pull and gather all the corners of the cheesecloth so that it hangs like a bag. Twist the cheesecloth to secure the curds and squeeze to release excess liquid. Shape it into a circle or block, and place under a heavy weight for about an hour (I use a saucepan filled with water). When all the whey is released, put the curds in the fridge with the cheesecloth. It will form a small block of paneer in about an hour or two. When the block is firm, the paneer is ready to use.* Discard the cheesecloth and cut the curds into 14–16 cubes.

**Serves 6 to 8.**

### Fun Fact

McDonald's in India makes a McSpicy Paneer Sandwich, a breaded slab of paneer on a bun with lettuce and creamy sauce. Or you can have a Spicy Paneer Wrap, a tortilla wrapped around grilled paneer with lettuce, tomato, onion, mustard, creamy sauce, and cheese.

# Achari Aloo (Mustard Potatoes) आचारी आलू

I adapted this recipe from my friend from Nepal, and it has now become our family favorite. These are potatoes with a twist, balancing complex flavors of sour, hot, and pungent (three of the six flavors of Ayurveda).

4 medium russet potatoes, whole and unpeeled

16 cups water (1 gallon)

3 tablespoons black sesame seeds

2 teaspoons cumin seeds

½ tablespoon black peppercorns

⅛ cup mustard oil

¼ cup vegetable oil

7 serrano chilies, sliced lengthwise*

1 tablespoon lime juice

1 tablespoon amchur powder

1 teaspoon turmeric powder

¾ tablespoon salt

Cilantro leaves

Place the potatoes in a Dutch oven, and fill with the water—it should be 3 inches above potatoes. Bring to a boil, cover, and cook for 20 to 25 minutes, or until tender but not falling apart.

Meanwhile, heat a small saucepan on medium-high, and dry-roast the sesame seeds, cumin seeds, and peppercorns. Stir constantly and roast for 4 minutes, or until the fragrances are released. In a coffee grinder or using a mortar and pestle, grind the roasted seeds to a powder and set aside.

Once the potatoes are cooked, peel and chop into 1 ½-inch chunks.

Heat a medium saucepan on high, and add the mustard oil and vegetable oil. Then add the serrano chilies and cook for 1 minute. Add the potatoes, and gently stir to coat the potatoes with the oil.

Add the reserved ground spices, then the lime juice, amchur powder, turmeric, and salt, and gently stir to coat potatoes. Serve hot.

Garnish with cilantro and serve with naan (see recipe on page 39).

**Serves 6 to 8.**

*If you like your dish less spicy, remove and discard the serrano seeds.

# Bundi Raita (Chickpea Flour Snacks in Yogurt) बूंदी रायता

An Indian meal is not complete without raita. Eat raita to cool and balance the palate when the heat of other foods is too much. Bundi are chickpea flour snacks available in Indian grocery stores.

4 cups plain yogurt

¾ tablespoon salt

1 ¼ cups bundi

1 teaspoon roasted cumin powder (or try Bina's Roasted Cumin)

½ teaspoon red chili powder or chaat masala

3 tablespoons chopped cilantro or mint leaves

In a medium bowl, beat the yogurt with the salt. Stir in the bundi and coat it with yogurt.

Add the cumin and chili powder or masala, and stir. Chill in the refrigerator. Before serving, stir and sprinkle with cilantro or mint to garnish.

Serve with rice, kebabs, chapattis, vegetables, and more!

**Serves 6 to 8.**

# *Naan* नान

In Persian, naan means "bread." This is the most famous leavened bread in North India, dry-roasted in earthen pots turned upside down. (They look like the huge pot that Alibaba hid in when he was being chased by the bad guy, Jaffar.) Many cultures in Central Asia and the Middle East have made a version of this bread since antiquity. In those days, they made it on an open fire pit made of bricks, and clay pots were buried in the ground. Traditionally, naan is cooked on the walls of a huge clay pot used as an oven called a tandoor. Be adventurous and create your own naan with different flavors, such as garlic, onion, or your favorite spices.

2 cups flour (all-purpose, whole wheat, or half-and-half) + ¼ cup for rolling

1 cup plain yogurt

¼ cup warm milk

2 tablespoons ghee

2 teaspoons salt

1 teaspoon sugar

¾ teaspoon baking powder

¼ teaspoon baking soda

2 tablespoons melted ghee

¼ cup kalonji seeds for presentation and flavor (optional)

Combine the 2 cups flour, the yogurt, milk, ghee, salt, sugar, baking powder, and baking soda in a bowl. Use your hands to mix and knead the ingredients together to form a smooth dough. Let the dough rest for 2 hours at room temperature, lightly covered.

Preheat the oven to 400 degrees when you are ready to cook the naan.

Break off 8 to 10 golf ball size pieces. Dip each piece in the ¼ cup flour for smooth rolling, and roll into an elongated shape like a teardrop (thinner at the top and wider at the bottom). Make each naan about 3 inches by 5 inches and ⅛ to ¼ inch thick.

Grease a cookie sheet, and place 2 naan pieces about 1 inch apart on the sheet.

Bake for 5 to 7 minutes. When brown spots appear, flip the naan over and cook for another 5 minutes, or until brown spots appear.

Remove from the oven and place on a cake cooling rack. While hot, brush with the melted ghee and sprinkle with kalonji seeds (if desired).

Continue baking naan until all the dough is used. Serve warm with all Indian dishes.

**Makes 8 to 10.**

Optional: Before baking the naan, top with finely chopped garlic.

Gujarat is the doorway to India, with a beautiful coastline on the Arabian Sea. Its strategic location, cultural heritage, and ethnic diversity are reflected in the region's food and lifestyle. A confluence of many religions—Hinduism, Buddhism, Jainism, and Islam—Gujarat also has been a home for minorities such as Parsis, Sindhis, Pathans, and Boris. Countless clans and tribes residing in the remote desert area of Kutch have also contributed to this rich and vibrant culture. Despite having diverse religious and ethnic beliefs, these people live in harmony and unity.

The region has been endowed with a profusion of vegetables, fruits, and lentils, and the cuisine reflects this, as well as the religion of the people who inhabit this area. Gujarat has perfected the art of vegetarian cuisine with emphasis on nutrition, consistency, flavor, and appearance. An endless repertoire of vegetarian options, the diversity of flavor, and the vibrancy of colors make the offerings far from monotonous.

The main meals are eaten on a metal platter, or thali. Thali also refers to a meal with many different dishes served in small bowls called katoris and arranged neatly on this platter. This is a visual treat. You eat with your eyes first before you take a mouthful!

From your first bite to your last, thali gives you many wonderful flavors, striking a unique balance of all six tastes of Ayurveda in one platter: pungent (pickles), sour (yogurt), salty (papads), sweet (shrikhand), astringent (potatoes and peas), and bitter (curry leaves). When all tastes are present in one meal, it is nutritionally sound and satisfying. The Gujarati thali culture has become so popular that you can now find regional variations in Indian restaurants all over the world.

In this menu, you'll find katoris of dahl, vegetables, yellow potatoes, green beans, eggplant, yogurt or salads, pickles, and papads served with a mound of rice and puris or rotlis in the center of the thali. The sweet dish shrikhand is served along with the meal in a katori, too. The meal is finished with a glass of spiced chaas or buttermilk (or lassi, as it is known in northern India) to help digestion. Enjoy the symphony of textures and tastes all on one plate.

# Chapter 2

# Gujarati Menu

Masala Puri                          44
Mung Dahl and Spinach                45
Corn Khees                           48
Potatoes and Peas                    49
Cauliflower and Peas                 50
Green Beans                          52
Spinach and Zucchini Raita           53
Shrikhand                            56
Pakora                               57

# *Masala Puri* मसाला पुरी

Like a sopapilla, a puri is deep-fried unleavened bread made with wheat flour and served as a snack with a cup of chai or coffee. It also can be served with vegetables and meat. It is considered party food or is for special occasions when you feel like indulging, since it is deep-fried. Masala refers to the spices, which give the bland dough a kick. Ajwain seeds (carom seeds) are an Ayurveda marvel with many digestive health benefits. In India, the water of this unassuming seed is given to babies every day for better digestion.

2 cups wheat flour

1 teaspoon turmeric powder

1 teaspoon red chili powder (optional)

1 teaspoon ajwain seeds (carom seeds)

1 tablespoon salt

3 tablespoons vegetable oil

1 ½ cups water

2 cups vegetable oil (for frying)

Combine the flour, turmeric, red chili powder (if desired), ajwain seeds, salt, and oil in a bowl and mix. Add the water, ½ cup at a time, to make a dough. The dough should be smooth and not too sticky. Don't worry if you add too much water—you can add a bit more flour to bring to a smooth consistency.

Grease your hands with oil and knead for 5 to 10 minutes, until a smooth, stiff dough forms. Let sit, covered, in a bowl for 30 minutes. Break off small pieces of the dough, around the size of a walnut, about 20 pieces. Roll out each piece 2 to 3 inches in diameter with a rolling pin (see photo).

In a large frying pan, heat the oil to between 350 and 375 degrees* (see also How to Deep-Fry on page 17).

With dry hands, gently place 2 to 3 flat puris into the oil one at a time (water and oil are not friends). Very lightly press the puri with the back of a slotted spoon to nudge it to puff. As soon as it puffs, immediately turn it over. Remove after 30 seconds with a slotted spoon. Allow the oil to drain and place on a paper towel to cool. Continue frying the remaining puris in batches.

**Serves 6 to 8.**

*For best results, the oil should be between 350 and 375 degrees. If not, the puris can turn soggy and greasy and won't puff up. If you do not have a thermometer, test the oil to see if it is ready. Drop a piece of the dough in the oil and see if the oil remains neutral or starts to bubble. The oil will be ready when the dough cooks in just a few seconds. Also, always make sure the oil does not smoke because this means it is burning and can cause the food to have an unpleasant odor.

# Mung Dahl and Spinach मुंग दाल और पालक

**I love this dish. Not only is it healthy—it's a vegetarian superfood meal—it's also a great option as a light evening soup or for a cleanse. It goes well with rice.**

1 cup yellow mung dahl

4 cups water (for soaking)

**Tempering ingredients (place each in separate small bowls)**

2 tablespoons vegetable oil

½ teaspoon mustard seeds

½ teaspoon cumin seeds

1 cinnamon stick

Pinch of hing

10–12 curry leaves (optional)

3 medium ripe tomatoes, finely chopped

½ teaspoon turmeric powder

1 teaspoon red chili powder

1 tablespoon salt

4 cups water

2 teaspoons garam masala (or try Bina's Garam Masala)

1 pound fresh spinach

Soak the mung dahl in the water for 1 hour before cooking or overnight.

*Tempering the ingredients:* Heat the oil in a large pot on medium-high. When the oil is hot, add the mustard and cumin seeds. When the seeds pop, immediately add the cinnamon and hing. Add the curry leaves (if desired), then the tomatoes and cook for 7 minutes, or until the tomatoes reduce or break down. Remove from the stove.

Drain the mung dahl and rinse. Add it to the tomato mixture. Stir in the turmeric, red chili powder, and salt, mixing well. Return the pot to the stove and cook on medium heat for 5 minutes, stirring continuously. Add the water and cook, uncovered, for 5 minutes, or until it comes to a boil. Reduce the heat to low, cover, and steam for 10 minutes.

Remove the lid, add the garam masala and spinach. Cook uncovered. Mix well for 1 to 2 minutes, or until the spinach wilts. Discard the cinnamon stick before serving.

**Serves 4 to 6.**

# Corn Khees मकाई खीस

Summer is when I go to the farmers' market and buy fresh corn. I enjoy making this dish when the corn has been picked right from the fields that morning. This is fantastic as a snack or side dish, and sometimes I use it as a filling for a panini with chutney. *Khees* means "to crush." In this recipe, I crush the fresh corn and spice it with herbs and tempered spices.

7 cups corn kernels, separated from cob and roughly chopped

1 ½ tablespoons salt

2 tablespoons grated ginger

1 teaspoon turmeric powder

**Tempering ingredients (place each in separate small bowls)**

½ cup ghee

½ teaspoon black mustard seeds

1 teaspoon cumin seeds

2 tablespoons finely diced serrano chilies

15 curry leaves

Pinch of hing

1 lime, juiced

½ cup finely chopped cilantro leaves

In a large bowl, mix together the corn, salt, ginger, and turmeric.

*Tempering the ingredients:* Heat a large pan on medium-high, then add the ghee. When the ghee is hot, add the mustard seeds and cumin seeds. Immediately after the seeds begin to pop, add the serrano chilies, curry leaves, and hing.

Quickly add the corn mixture to the tempered spices. Mix well and cook, stirring constantly, for 10 to 15 minutes, until sizzling hot.

Garnish with lime and chopped cilantro and serve hot.

**Serves 6 to 8.**

# Potatoes and Peas आलू और मटर

I make this every other week in the summer, because so many of the ingredients are fresh, especially the tomatoes that come straight off the vine. I love this with puris or as a soup. In winter, I add tomato paste to this recipe to enhance the flavor of the tomatoes.

4 medium potatoes, peeled and diced into 1-inch cubes

1 green bell pepper, diced small

½ cup chopped mint leaves

2 cups frozen peas

1 ½ tablespoons salt

2 teaspoons turmeric powder

2 tablespoons ground coriander

1 tablespoon red chili powder

5 medium tomatoes, diced, or 1 can (20 ounces) crushed tomatoes

1 serrano chili, diced small

**Tempering ingredients (place each in separate small bowls)**

3 tablespoons ghee or vegetable oil

1 teaspoon black mustard seeds

¼ teaspoon fenugreek seeds (methi)

Pinch of hing

10 curry leaves

3 cups water

1 tablespoon tomato paste (optional in winter or when fresh tomatoes are not available)

1 tablespoon sugar (optional)

Place the potatoes, bell pepper, and mint in a large bowl. Add the peas, salt, turmeric, coriander, and red chili powder and set aside.

In a separate bowl, combine the tomatoes, and serrano chili.

*Tempering the ingredients:* Heat the ghee or oil on medium-high in a deep cooking pot. When the oil is hot, add the black mustard seeds and fenugreek seeds. When the seeds start to pop, add the hing and curry leaves.

Immediately add the tomato mixture and cook for 8 minutes, until they break down. Turn the heat up to high. Add the potato mixture and cook for 3 minutes, mixing well.

Add the water and allow the mixture to come to a boil. Turn the heat to medium-low and simmer, covered, for 25 minutes, or until the potatoes are fully cooked. Mix in the tomato paste and sugar (if desired) and simmer for 2 minutes, or until hot.

**Serves 6 to 8.**

# Cauliflower and Peas फूल गोबी और मटर

This is a perfect side dish for a vegetarian, served with dahl and rice. Simple, quick, and easy to make, it can also be served with kebabs, breads, or quinoa. I have made this dish countless times for my family and friends, and they love it, but my son-in-law especially loves it.

1 medium cauliflower, florets separated

1 cup frozen peas

1 large bell pepper, diced into small pieces

1 tablespoon grated ginger

1 tablespoon fennel seeds

2 teaspoons turmeric powder

1 tablespoon ground coriander

1 teaspoon red chili powder

1 tablespoon salt

**Tempering ingredients (place each in separate small bowls)**

⅓ cup ghee or vegetable oil

½ teaspoon cumin seeds

½ teaspoon mustard seeds

¼ teaspoon hing

1 serrano chili, sliced

10–12 curry leaves (optional)

1 tablespoon lime juice

2 tablespoons chopped cilantro leaves

Place the cauliflower, peas, and bell pepper in a bowl. Add the ginger, fennel seeds, turmeric, coriander, red chili powder, and salt and mix well. Set aside.

*Tempering the ingredients:* Heat the ghee or oil on medium-high in a 3-quart saucepan. Once the oil is hot, add the cumin seeds and mustard seeds. As soon as the seeds start popping, add the hing, serrano chili, and curry leaves (if desired).

Immediately add the vegetable mixture to the tempered ingredients. Mix thoroughly, cover, and cook on medium heat for 10 minutes. If you want it al dente, cook for 8 minutes.

Before serving, stir the lime juice into the mixture and garnish with cilantro.

Serve with chapattis, naan, puris, or raita.

**Serves 6 to 8.**

# Green Beans हरी फन्सी

I grew up with this recipe—it's a very typical Gujarati dish that was made in my home at least three times a week. This is great to make in the summertime when the green beans are fresh off the vine. It's also very simple to make, is extremely light, is a good diet food, and would be good for a detox or cleanse if you're doing such a program. Tip: The pinch of baking soda keeps the greens green—but more than a pinch will ruin the taste!

5 cups chopped green beans, ends removed

Pinch of baking soda

1 ¼ tablespoons salt

1 tablespoon grated ginger

1 tablespoon serrano chilies, finely blended in food processor

**Tempering ingredients (place each in separate small bowls)**

2 teaspoons ghee or vegetable oil

½ teaspoon ajwain seeds (carom seeds)

Pinch of hing

6 cups water

1 tablespoon salt

1 tablespoon lime juice

Cilantro leaves

Place the green beans in a bowl with the baking soda. Add the salt, ginger, and serrano chili paste, and mix well. Set aside.

*Tempering the ingredients:* Heat the ghee or oil on medium-high in a 3-quart saucepan. Once the oil is hot, add the ajwain seeds. When the seeds start to pop, add the hing, green bean mixture, water, and salt and bring to a boil uncovered. Cook for 10 to 15 minutes.

Garnish with the lime juice and cilantro and serve.

**Serves 4 to 6.**

# Spinach and Zucchini Raita पालक और ज़ुकिनी रायता

Cooling, alkalizing, and healthy, this makes a wonderful breakfast or light lunch. My sister-in-law taught me how to make this dish. The tempering of the kalonji seeds, or onion seeds, makes this an exotic-tasting raita.

1 cup baby spinach

Pinch of baking soda

1 zucchini (grated and drained)

1 ¼ teaspoons salt (divided)

3 cups plain yogurt

3 whole green onions with tops, finely diced

½ teaspoon finely diced serrano chilies (optional)

1 teaspoon roasted cumin powder (or try Bina's Roasted Cumin)

**Tempering ingredients (place each in separate small bowls)**

2 teaspoons ghee or vegetable oil

½ teaspoon kalonji seeds (onion seeds)

Pinch of hing (optional)

Wash the spinach and soak in a bowl of water with the baking soda for 5 minutes. Drain and chop finely.

Grate the zucchini in a separate bowl, mix in ¼ teaspoon of the salt, and let sit for 5 to 7 minutes. Press in a colander to remove excess liquid. This will prevent the raita from becoming too runny.

Place the spinach, zucchini, yogurt, green onions, and serrano chilies (if desired) in a large bowl and mix. Add the cumin and the remaining 1 teaspoon salt to the mixture and stir. Set aside.

*Tempering the ingredients:* Heat the ghee or oil on medium-high in a 1-quart saucepan. Once the oil is hot, add the kalonji seeds. When the seeds start to pop, add the hing (if desired) and remove from the stove. Add to the bowl with the spinach mixture and thoroughly combine. Refrigerate until ready and serve cold.

**Serves 6 to 8.**

# Shrikhand  श्रीखंड

My friend Karel calls this "ambrosia," a food fit for the gods. This is a yogurt-based sweet dish served at big festivals, prayer ceremonies, and special celebrations. In Gujarat, desserts are served together with the main meal. You can also put this in an ice cream maker and create a divine frozen yogurt.

32 ounces (1 quart) plain Greek yogurt

1 cup sugar or monk fruit sweetener

2 teaspoons saffron

1 tablespoon cardamom powder

3 tablespoons crushed pistachios and/or almonds (optional)

1 teaspoon rose water (optional)

In a bowl, mix the yogurt, sugar, saffron, cardamom, nuts (if desired), and rose water (if desired). Allow the mixture to marinate in the refrigerator overnight or until an orange color sets in. Mix well before serving.

**Serves 6 to 8.**

# *Pakora* पकोड़ा

Pakora, or bhajia, is an Indian version of vegetable tempura. It is a gluten-free vegan dish that is comforting on a cold winter's day and especially fun to have as a snack during cocktail hour. Serve these with any of my delicious chutneys (see pages 195-202). It will be divine!

## Batter

2 cups besan (chickpea flour)

2 tablespoons rice flour

3 cups water

1 tablespoon salt

1 tablespoon ground coriander

2 teaspoons red chili powder

1 teaspoon turmeric powder

1 teaspoon ground black pepper

½ teaspoon ajwain seeds (carom seeds)

½ teaspoon baking powder

1 teaspoon sunflower oil

## Veggies

4 cups vegetable oil

1 small eggplant, cut into ¼-inch slices

1 cup cauliflower florets, cut into 2-inch pieces

1 small sweet potato, peeled and cut into ¼-inch slices

1 small zucchini, cut into ¾-inch slices

1 medium onion, cut into ¼-inch slices

*To make the batter:* Mix the besan, rice flour, water, salt, coriander, red chili powder, turmeric, black pepper, ajwain seeds, baking powder, and sunflower oil in a medium bowl. Stir until all the lumps are well incorporated.

*To make the veggies:* Heat the oil in a deep skillet to 350–375 degrees. To test the oil for readiness, add a drop of the batter to the pan. If it starts to sizzle and float to the top immediately, it is ready for deep-frying (see How to Deep-Fry on page 17).

Dip a few of the vegetables in the batter by hand, coat well with batter, and allow the batter to drain off. Place the battered vegetables one at a time in the hot oil and cook for 3 to 5 minutes, or until golden brown. Cook in small batches. Serve hot with your favorite chutney.

**Serves 6 to 8.**

I was born and raised in Bombay—or Mumbai, as it known today—an exuberant city that never sleeps, teeming and beaming with life. Inspired by the mélange of cultures, communities, tribes, and religions there, street food is an integral part of the city's culture and a way of life. Affordable and available on every corner, Mumbai street food transcends barriers of caste, creed, and customs. Here we experience cultural harmony and unity on our palates.

You'll find hot, healthy options that are nourishing and tasty, along with sweet or fried indulgences that are decadent and luscious. Available all hours of the day and night, street food is comfort food—from a simple bag of roasted peanuts to indulgent samosas, potato pattice, and pakoras. You'll find grilled meats such as the complex kebabs at Mohammed Ali Road, fish specialties at Trishna, grilled chicken at Bademiya. If it is vegetarian options you're craving, you'll find pani puri (golgappas) at Chowpatty Beach, chole puri at the Cream Centre, vada pav, paav bhaji, and idlis served with sambhar at Swati Snacks on Kemps Corner. For a special treat, don't miss the kulfi centers—Indian ice cream vendors touting every flavor. For an afternoon pick-me-up, cutting chai is sold on every street corner in two-ounce paper cups. I have my favorite chaiwallahs (people who sell chai), and visiting them is the first thing I do when I'm in this city.

I love the movie *The Hundred-Foot Journey*, which reveals the essence and pride of Indian cooking with spices and fresh foods. With my recipes, you can take your own hundred-foot journey through the streets of Mumbai and bring the rhythms, tastes, and sounds of its incredible street food into your own home. Be adventurous, and savor these culinary delights!

# Chapter 3

# Bombay Street Food

| | |
|---|---|
| Samosa | 61 |
| Hariyali Chicken Kebabs | 64 |
| Pani Puri | 65 |
| Vadaa Paav | 68 |
| Paav Bhaji | 71 |
| Authentic Indian Chai | 73 |

# Samosa समोसा

Samosas are a popular street food in Mumbai and have gained fame worldwide. My recipe includes all six tastes plus the crunch. The potatoes are the sweet taste; the lime is the sour; the cumin and coriander are the bitter; the ginger and chilies are the pungent; the turmeric and cilantro are the astringent; and, of course, salt is the salty taste. Once the samosas are fried, they have an amazing crunch. It's no wonder this treat satisfies the mind, body, and spirit. I've offered the potato filling here, but there are many different types of fillings you can make, including meat.

## Filling

5 large russet potatoes (3 ¼ pounds), whole and unpeeled

3 tablespoons ground coriander

1 tablespoon ground black pepper

1 ¼ tablespoons roasted cumin powder (or try Bina's Roasted Cumin)

½ teaspoon turmeric powder

2 teaspoons red chili powder

1 tablespoon garam masala (or try Bina's Garam Masala)

2 tablespoons amchur powder

1 tablespoon salt

⅓ cup ghee or sunflower oil

1 tablespoon small-diced serrano chilies (about 2)

2 tablespoons grated ginger

2 cups peas

½ cup chopped cilantro leaves

½ tablespoon lime juice

## Pastry

5 cups all-purpose flour

2 tablespoons uncooked Cream of Wheat

1 tablespoon salt

1 teaspoon ajwain seeds (carom seeds)

2 cups water (divided)

2 ½ tablespoons ghee

2 tablespoons sunflower oil

Flour for rolling

4 cups vegetable oil for deep frying

*To make the filling:* Put the potatoes in a 10-quart saucepan, and fill with water until 4 inches above the potatoes. Boil the potatoes, covered, for 40 to 50 minutes, or until soft when poked with a fork (or use a pressure cooker, following directions).

While the potatoes are boiling, measure the coriander, black pepper, cumin, turmeric, red chili powder, garam masala, amchur powder, and salt into a bowl and set aside.

Remove the potatoes from the water and let cool enough to be handled. Peel the potatoes by rubbing the skin off with your fingers. Skins should slide off easily. Discard the skins and place the potatoes in a large bowl. While warm, coarsely mash them with a potato masher.

Heat the ghee or oil in a 10-quart saucepan on medium-high. Add the serrano chilies, ginger, and peas and saute for 1 to 2 minutes. Add the mashed potatoes and mix well. Add the reserved spice

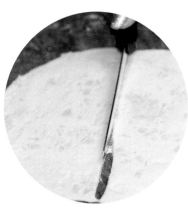

mixture, cilantro, and lime juice, and mix well. Allow the mixture to cool before filling samosa shells.

*To make the pastry:* Mix the all-purpose flour, Cream of Wheat, salt, and ajwain in a large bowl. Add 1 cup of the water, the ghee, and sunflower oil.

Sprinkle all-purpose flour on a flat surface and knead the dough with your palms, using a pushing motion, for 3 to 5 minutes, or until smooth. Add the remaining 1 cup water a little at a time, until all of the flour is well incorporated. The dough should be pliable and on the soft side, but not wet. Use your judgment when adding water. If you add too much water and the dough is sticky, add a bit more flour. Put the dough in a large bowl, cover, and let sit for 30 minutes to rest.

Break off a piece of dough about the size of a walnut and roll it between your palms into a ball, making sure there are no cracks. On the floured surface, use a rolling pin to roll the ball into a thin, round circle, 4–5 inches in diameter and ⅛ inch thick. Cut the circle in half. Lightly moisten the edges with water and join two edges together to make a cone (see photo). Put about one spoonful of cooled samosa filling in the pastry cone.

Moisten the exposed top edges and seal by pinching them together. Continue this process with all of the dough and filling.

Heat the vegetable oil in a Dutch oven or wok (kadhai) on medium-high until the temperature is 350–375 degrees (see How to Deep-Fry on page 17). Oil must be hot but not smoking before frying, and it must maintain the same temperature. To test the oil for readiness, drop a small piece of the pastry dough in the oil. If the dough starts to sizzle and floats to the top, it is ready.

Add 3 to 5 samosas at a time to the oil. Cook for 3 to 5 minutes, or until golden brown, flip over, and cook for another 3 to 5 minutes. Drain with a slotted spoon or metal spider skimmer (see page 19), and place on paper towels to remove excess oil. Repeat this process until all the samosas are fried. Samosas can be stored in the refrigerator for up to 5 days.

Serve with Green Pecan Chutney (recipe on page 199) and Amchur Chutney (recipe on page 199).

**Makes 16 to 18.**

# Hariyali Chicken Kebabs हरियाली मुर्ग कबाब

Also called "Green Chicken" because they're made with green herbs, these kebabs are a roadside favorite in Mumbai, where people wait in queues to eat this mouthwatering treat served with naan. The dry-roasted spices are a delicious blend that can be made ahead of time. Double or triple the spice recipe, and store this blend in a sealed glass jar for future use. Kebabs are delicious grilled, but they can also be prepared ahead for a cold picnic as a main dish by itself or in a wrap with raita, chutney, and caramelized onions.

**Dry-roasted spices**

6 tablespoons coriander seeds

4 tablespoons black peppercorns

2 tablespoons cumin seeds

1 teaspoon ajwain seeds (carom seeds)

**Marinade**

1 large bunch cilantro leaves

1 large bunch mint leaves

3 green onions with tops

1 tablespoon sesame oil

2 tablespoons vegetable oil

2 tablespoons mustard oil

¼ cup water

1 serrano chili

¼ cup lime juice

2 teaspoons salt (or to taste)

10 cloves garlic

1 small piece of ginger

4 pounds boneless, skinless chicken breasts and thighs, cut into 2-inch pieces

2 large onions, cut into large chunks

*To make the dry-roasted spices:* Heat a medium skillet over medium-high and add the coriander, peppercorns, cumin, and ajwain. Roast for 2 to 3 minutes, or until fragrant, shaking the skillet constantly so they do not burn. Transfer to a small bowl, and allow them to come to room temperature before grinding in a coffee grinder to a smooth powder.

*To make the marinade:* In a blender or food processor, add the cilantro, mint, green onions, sesame oil, vegetable oil, mustard oil, water, serrano chili, lime juice, salt, garlic, and ginger. Blend to make a smooth paste. Add the dry-roasted spices and mix well.

Place the mixture in a plastic bag or sealed container (I like to use plastic bags so I can massage the marinade into the meat), and add the chicken. Let marinate in the refrigerator for 4 to 6 hours.

Before grilling, bring the chicken to room temperature. Alternate the chicken pieces and onion pieces on a skewer.

Spray the grates with cooking oil and preheat the grill to high. When it's hot, place the skewers in the middle of the grill where it is the hottest. Sear the chicken on high for 30 seconds to 1 minute on all sides to seal in the juices. Reduce the heat to medium and continue grilling the chicken, covered, 6 minutes on each side. The meat should reach 165 degrees; use a thermometer for optimal results.

**Serves 8.**

# *Pani Puri* पाणि पुरी

Pani puri is one of the most popular street foods in all of India. The pani is a spicy liquid for dunking the puri, a tiny crispy pastry filled with potato, mung, and chana. The sprouted mung beans and chickpeas are very healthy because of their vitamins and minerals, and pani has excellent digestive qualities. It's a great meal, and it's fun to eat.

To simplify this dish, sprout the beans ahead of time and purchase pani puri shells at an Indian grocery store.

### Sprouting

2 cups black chana (black chickpeas)

9 cups water (divided)

1 cup whole mung beans

### Filling

2 medium potatoes, whole and unpeeled

1 teaspoon chaat masala (or try Bina's Bombay Masala)

1 teaspoon salt

### Pani water

3 cups mint leaves

1 tablespoon black peppercorns

1 tablespoon cumin seeds

1 tablespoon coriander seeds

4 serrano chilies

½ inch piece of ginger

1 lime, juiced

2 tablespoons tamarind paste (or to taste), or 2 slices green mango in season

10 cups water (divided)

2 tablespoons black salt (sanchal)

1 tablespoon salt (or to taste)

1 teaspoon roasted cumin powder (or try Bina's Roasted Cumin)

2 boxes of 30 puri shells (purchase at an Indian grocery store)

Amchur Chutney (recipe on page 199)

*To sprout:* In two large bowls, soak the chana in 5 cups water and the mung beans in 4 cups water for 8 to 12 hours, or overnight. The beans will expand as they absorb the water. Drain and rinse the soaked beans.

*continued on page 67*

*continued from page 65*

Place the beans in two separate moistened cheesecloths or breathable cotton cloths, and tie at the ends. Then place them in separate bowls and set in a dark place. Every 6 hours, rinse the beans in their cloth bundles and thoroughly drain all water before returning them to the dark place to continue sprouting. The beans should be moist but not sitting in standing water. In 1 to 2 days, they will germinate.

Once sprouted, separately boil the chana for 20 minutes and the mung beans for 5 minutes. Cooking time begins once the water starts boiling. Drain, cool, and set aside.

*To make the filling:* Put the potatoes in a 10-quart saucepan, and fill with water until 4 inches above the potatoes. Boil, covered, for 20 to 30 minutes, or until soft when poked with a fork (or use a pressure cooker, following directions).

Remove from the water and let cool until the potatoes can be handled. Peel the potatoes by rubbing the skin off with your fingers. Skins should slide off easily. Discard the skins and place the potatoes in a large bowl. While warm, coarsely mash them with a potato masher. Sprinkle with the masala and salt. Set aside.

*To make the pani water:* In a blender, place the mint, peppercorns, cumin, coriander, serrano chilies, ginger, lime juice, and tamarind paste or mango with ½ cup of the water. Blend to form a smooth paste. Add the remaining 9 ½ cups water, the black salt, salt, and cumin and blend. Chill for 3 to 4 hours. Strain and discard the solids. Store the pani water in a glass container.

To assemble: Serve as a thali by putting the filling, sprouted mung, and sprouted chana in small dishes and the pani in a larger bowl. Make a hole in the center of each puri. Add ½ teaspoon mung and ½ teaspoon chana. Add 1 small spoonful of potato filling. Add ¼ teaspoon of the Amchur Chutney.

Dunk the filled puri in the pani and put the whole thing in your mouth. Enjoy.

**Makes 60; serves 6 to 8.**

*Sprouted beans can be stored in plastic bags or sealed containers in the refrigerator for up to 7 days. Two cups of black chana make 3 cups once sprouted. One cup of mung beans makes 3 cups once sprouted. The weather can determine how quickly they sprout.*

# Vadaa Paav वडा पाव

Vadaa paav is a fast-food vegetarian burger. Many workers and commuters have short lunch breaks, so a vadaa paav is a quick, easy, and tasty meal that satisfies hunger. The dish evolved in Bombay and has now migrated across India. Serve with sliced raw onion, Garlic Chutney (recipe on page 200), and Green Pecan Chutney (recipe on page 199).

## Potatoes

4 potatoes, whole and unpeeled

2 tablespoons grated ginger

1 tablespoon small-diced serrano chilies

1 teaspoon turmeric powder

1 tablespoon salt

1 teaspoon sugar

½ teaspoon red chili powder (optional)

1 lemon, juiced

1 cup finely chopped cilantro leaves

## Batter

2 cups besan (chickpea flour)

2 tablespoons rice flour

3 cups water

1 tablespoon salt

1 tablespoon ground coriander

2 teaspoons red chili powder

1 teaspoon turmeric powder

½ teaspoon ground black pepper

½ teaspoon ajwain seeds (carom seeds)

½ teaspoon baking powder

## Deep-frying

6 cups vegetable oil

Hamburger buns

Ghee

Garlic Chutney (recipe on page 200)

Green Pecan Chutney (recipe on page 199)

Sliced onions

Cilantro leaves

## Tempering ingredients (place each in separate small bowls)

2 tablespoons vegetable oil

½ teaspoon mustard seeds

¼ teaspoon urad dahl, split and husked (or white dahl; see Dahl Chart on page 12)

10–12 curry leaves

Pinch of hing

*To make the potatoes:* Put the potatoes in a 10-quart saucepan, and fill with water until 4 inches above the potatoes. Boil, covered, for 20 to 30 minutes, or until soft when poked with a fork (or use a pressure cooker, following directions).

Remove from the water and let cool until they can be handled. Peel the potatoes by rubbing the skin off with your fingers.

*continued on page 70*

*continued from page 68*

Skins should slide off easily. Discard the skins and place the potatoes in a large bowl. While warm, coarsely mash them with a potato masher. Add the ginger, serrano chilies, turmeric, salt, sugar, red chili powder (if desired), lemon juice, and cilantro. Mix well.

*Tempering the ingredients:* Heat the oil in a small frying pan over medium-high. Once the oil is hot, add mustard seeds, urad dahl, and curry leaves. Once the seeds start to pop, add the hing.

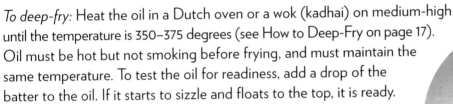

Add the tempered spices to the potatoes and mix well. Form the mixture into 3-inch potato patties (like a small hamburger).

*To make the batter:* Mix the besan, rice flour, water, salt, coriander, red chili powder, turmeric, black pepper, ajwain seeds, and baking powder in a medium bowl. Stir until all the lumps are gone.

*To deep-fry:* Heat the oil in a Dutch oven or a wok (kadhai) on medium-high until the temperature is 350–375 degrees (see How to Deep-Fry on page 17). Oil must be hot but not smoking before frying, and must maintain the same temperature. To test the oil for readiness, add a drop of the batter to the oil. If it starts to sizzle and floats to the top, it is ready.

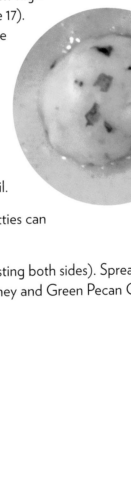

Dip the potato patties in the batter and allow the excess batter to drain off. Place the patties in the hot oil one at a time. Cook for 3 to 5 minutes, or until golden brown on one side, then flip it over and cook the other side for 3 to 5 minutes. Drain with a slotted spoon or metal spider skimmer, and place on paper towels to remove excess oil.

Repeat this process until all the vadaa paav are fried. The cooked patties can be stored in the refrigerator for up to 5 days.

To assemble: Toast the hamburger buns in a toaster or on a grill (toasting both sides). Spread ghee on the buns and place a patty on one side. Top with the Garlic Chutney and Green Pecan Chutney. Garnish with onions and cilantro and enjoy!

**Serves 6 to 8.**

# Paav Bhaji पाव भाजी

This "poor man's food" is a recipe actually developed by a poor man who is now a rich man because of his delicious invention that became wildly popular all over India. Available in Mumbai's financial district, paav bhaji is eaten and served like a sloppy joe! Toppings could include raw onions, squeezed lemon, and cilantro. Adjust the amount of spices to your taste and preference. The paav bhaji spice mix is available in Indian grocery stores.

2 medium potatoes, whole and unpeeled

1 teaspoon turmeric powder

3 tablespoons ground coriander

½ teaspoon red chili powder

1 tablespoon salt

4 tablespoons paav bhaji masala (Badshah brand)

4 tablespoons ghee, plus extra for spreading on the buns

2 ½ cups finely chopped onions

2 cloves garlic, finely minced

1 cup finely chopped cauliflower

¾ cup finely chopped bell peppers

½ cup peas

1 can (28 ounces) crushed tomatoes

1 cup finely chopped cilantro leaves

Hamburger buns

Put the potatoes in a 10-quart saucepan, and fill with water until 4 inches above the potatoes. Boil, covered, for 20 to 30 minutes, or until soft when poked with a fork (or use a pressure cooker, following directions).

Remove from the water and cool until the potatoes can be handled. Peel the potatoes by rubbing the skin off with your fingers. Skins should slide off easily. Discard the skins and place in a large bowl. While warm, coarsely mash them with a potato masher.

Measure the turmeric, coriander, red chili powder, salt, and masala into a small bowl.

Melt the ghee in a 6-quart saucepan. Add the onions and cook on medium-high for 10 to 12 minutes, or until translucent. Add the garlic and sauté for 1 minute. Add the cauliflower, bell peppers, and peas. Cook until soft. Add the tomatoes and cook for 10 to 12 minutes, or until the water is reduced and the tomatoes break down.

Add the potatoes and spices, and mix well. Simmer for 5 minutes. Add the cilantro and mix well.

Spread the hamburger buns with ghee (or butter) and place on a hot griddle. Flatten the buns with a spatula and allow the bread to get crispy. Pour the potato mixture on the bread and enjoy!

**Serves 6 to 8.**

# Authentic Indian Chai  चाय

Chai is a drink India cannot live without. *Chai* means tea, and a chaiwallah is the vendor who sells chai. In India, this popular drink made with milk, spices, and sugar is more than just a cup of tea to wake up to every day. It is deeply ingrained in the culture of India as a ritual and rhythm of life. India's chai culture transcends all boundaries as the one unifying presence in a profoundly diverse country.

Like Starbucks, chaiwallahs are found anywhere and everywhere—in small stalls on the street or as wandering vendors yelling "chai, wallah, chai!" at railway stations and other locations. People gather around the crude stoves, heated by coal, from early morning to late evening to drink chai and exchange news and gossip. It's the least expensive thing you can buy on the street and is enjoyed by everyone—young and old, rich and poor—because it is a way of life.

4 cups water

1 tablespoon grated ginger

1 cup whole milk*

4 teaspoons black tea

1 tablespoon chai masala

2 tablespoons sugar (optional)

In a 4-quart stainless steel saucepan on high heat, bring the water and ginger to a boil. Add the milk, black tea, chai masala, and sugar (if desired) and bring to a boil again. Take it off the stove immediately, strain the mixture, and serve in cups.

**Serves 4.**

*If you choose to substitute almond, cashew, or soy milk, you will need to use 4 cups of it and reduce the water to 1 cup. Do not use coconut milk because it will separate while heating.

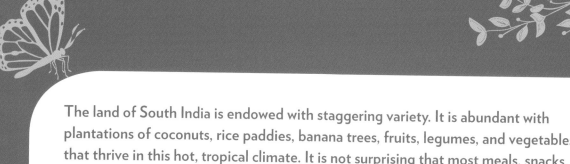

The land of South India is endowed with staggering variety. It is abundant with plantations of coconuts, rice paddies, banana trees, fruits, legumes, and vegetables that thrive in this hot, tropical climate. It is not surprising that most meals, snacks, and recipes are made with rice, bananas, and coconuts in every form. The area is famous for its spice plantations that grow cardamom, cinnamon, clove, ginger, vanilla, nutmeg, black pepper, ginger, oregano, rosemary, curry leaves, thyme, holy basil (tulsi), mint, bay leaves, coriander, mustard seeds, peppercorns, fenugreek, chilies, and tamarind.

Adding to the allure of this and the lush, green landscape, there are many Ayurvedic centers that attract visitors worldwide. Ayurveda philosophy recognizes the medicinal and healing powers of all-natural herbs, spices, seeds, and oils, which are key to reducing inflammation, improving metabolism and digestion, and boosting immunity, helping people to live a pain-free and joyful life. It is no wonder that this region has spawned many Ayurvedic centers where qualified Ayurvedic doctors and nutritionists offer programs for cleanses, rejuvenation, and revitalization of digestion that are affordable. A few years ago, I had the privilege of experiencing a 14-day program in one of these centers, and I had an amazing rejuvenation and revitalizing experience.

The traditional food of South India is the hottest food of all Indian foods. The ghost pepper is native to this region. South Indian foods such as dosas and idlis are easily digestible due to the fermenting process and are considered tridoshic. The fermenting process increases the quick absorption of vitamins, minerals, and macronutrients found in the lentils and grains used in this cuisine. I love these and have offered choices in my South Indian menu. One of my favorite things to do in this region is to finish my meal with coffee that is sold outside the many temples found here. This coffee is made with chicory, sugar, and cardamom mixed with frothed and boiled milk.

The fermented batters I include (see Fermenting on page 13) require planning since fermentation takes a few days. Initially, it involves a little effort, but the batters can be stored in the fridge for 5 to 10 days for quicker use. These dishes are not only delicious but also nourishing and easily digestible.

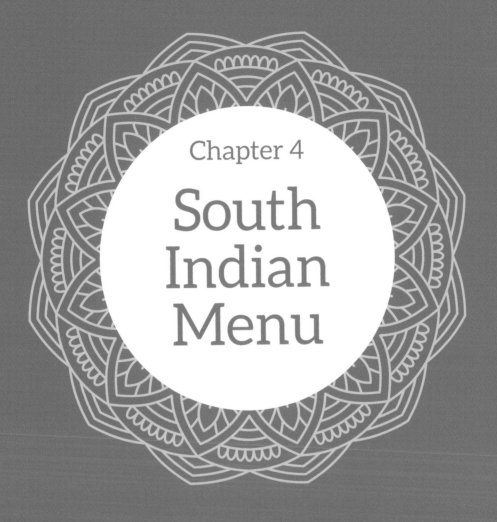

# Chapter 4

# South Indian Menu

Traditional Dosa                 78
Mung Dahl Dosa                   79
Idli                             82
Rasam                            83
Sambhar                          86
Potato Filling for Dosa          87
Karam Podi                       89
Chettinad Curry                  90

# Traditional Dosa डोसा

When I first came to the United States, I yearned for some of my favorite dishes and especially dosas. Dosas are crispy, savory, papery, gluten-free crepes often served with chutneys, karam podis, potato filling, sambhar, and rasam. I was thrilled when a neighbor from Nepal made me dosas to satisfy my cravings. My family thinks it is funny that I learned how to make the best dosas from a Nepalese woman living in Colorado. This popular street food is now found all over India, but it is indigenous to South India.

3 cups uncooked white rice (jasmine or long-grain)

1 cup split urad dahl (or white dahl; see Dahl Chart on page 12)

¼ cup chana dahl

½ teaspoon fenugreek seeds (methi)

2 cups reserved water from soaked dahl

2 tablespoons salt

⅓ cup coconut oil or vegetable oil (do not use olive oil)

**Dosas pair well with Sambhar (recipe on page 86) and Coconut Chutney (recipe on page 202).**

Rinse the rice, urad dahl, and chana dahl separately and drain. Place the rice, dahls, and fenugreek seeds in a large bowl and add enough water to cover by 4 inches. Soak for at least 10 hours or overnight. The dahls and rice will expand.

Drain the water, reserving 2 cups. Place the drained ingredients in small batches in a blender and blend to make a smooth, thick batter, adding a little water as needed if the mixture gets too thick. Add the salt and mix well.

Store the batter in a large bowl covered with a breathable cloth. Put in a warm place to ferment where it won't be disturbed. Place a cookie sheet or cloth underneath, in case the mixture overflows.

Ferment for 12 to 24 hours, depending on the season, or until the batter appears to have doubled in size and bubbles appear. (The hotter the temperature outside, the less time it will need to ferment. In the winter, it will require at least 36 hours but no more than 48 hours. See Fermenting on page 13.) Once fermented, this batter can be used for 10 to 15 days when stored in the refrigerator in a sealed container.

Preheat a nonstick griddle or pan on high, and wipe the pan with a wet cloth. (Note: Do not put oil on the pan before adding the batter.) When the pan is hot, reduce the heat to medium-high and pour in ⅓ cup of the batter in a circular motion to make a 6- to 8-inch dosa, like a crepe. Sprinkle a little bit of coconut or vegetable oil on top as it cooks. This will allow the dosa to get crispy.

When it starts to turn brown, fold the dosa in half, pressing it lightly with the spatula. The dosa only needs to be cooked on one side. Before folding, you can add the Potato Filling for Dosas (recipe on page 87). Repeat with the remaining batter.

**Serves 8 to 10.**

# Mung Dahl Dosa मूग डोसा

This pancake is made only with yellow split lentils, so it is grain-free. The batter is fermented, like dosas, but it ferments much faster, in 6 to 8 hours. Mung Dahl Dosas can be used in many cleanses, and it is good for all three body types (vata, pitta, and kapha). It is served with a wide variety of sauces, sides, and fillings. New York's SoHo District serves dosas with fillings and sauces from around the world. Use your imagination!

2 cups mung dahl (yellow split lentils)

½ cup split urad dahl (or white dahl; see Dahl Chart on page 12)

¼ cup uncooked white rice (jasmine or long-grain)

½ teaspoon fenugreek seeds (methi)

2 cups reserved water from soaked dahl

1 tablespoon salt (or to taste)

⅓ cup coconut oil or vegetable oil (do not use olive oil)

Rinse the mung dahl, urad dahl, and rice separately and drain. Place the dahls, rice, and fenugreek seeds in a large bowl and add enough water to cover by 4 inches. Soak for at least 10 hours or overnight. The dahls and rice will expand.

Drain the water, reserving 2 cups. Place the drained ingredients in small batches in a blender and blend to make a smooth, thick batter, adding a little water as needed. Stir in the salt.

Put the batter in a large bowl covered with a breathable cloth. Place it in a warm place where it won't be disturbed. Place a cookie sheet or cloth underneath in case the mixture overflows during the fermentation process.

Ferment for 6 to 8 hours, or until bubbles appear in the batter. (See Fermenting on page 13.) Once fermented, this batter can be used for about 2 days when stored in the refrigerator in a sealed container.

Preheat a nonstick griddle or pan on high, and wipe the pan with a wet cloth. (Note: Do not put oil on the pan before adding the batter.) When the pan is hot, reduce the heat to medium-high and pour in ⅓ cup of the batter in a circular motion to make a 6- to 8-inch dosa, like a crepe. Sprinkle a little bit of coconut or vegetable oil on top as it cooks. This will allow the dosa to get crispy.

When it starts to turn brown, fold the dosa in half, pressing it lightly with the spatula. The dosa only needs to be cooked on one side. Repeat with the remaining batter. Dosas are accompanied with chutneys, karam podi, potato filling, sambhar, and rasam.

**Serves 8 to 10.**

# Idli (Steamed Rice Cakes) इडली

Idlis are tridoshic, which means they are good for any body type (vata, pitta, or kapha). Idlis are a traditional South Indian breakfast favorite and have gained popularity in just about any breakfast buffet across India and Sri Lanka. These are steamed cakes made with fermented lentils and rice. Fermentation is a main component in making idlis soft. You'll need an idlis steamer with molds (available online or in East Indian grocery stores) or a 9-piece egg poacher set.

2 cups uncooked
long-grain rice

1 cup split urad dahl (or
white dahl; see Dahl Chart
on page 12)

2 cups reserved water from
soaked dahl

1 tablespoon salt

Oil or cooking spray

Rinse the rice and urad dahl separately, place in separate bowls, and add enough water to cover by 4 inches. Soak for at least 9 hours or overnight.

Drain the dahl, reserving 2 cups of the water. Place the dahl and ¼ cup of the reserved water in a blender and blend into a smooth, thick paste. The batter should be thick, but if it's too thick, add water ¼ cup at a time. Remove and set aside.

Drain the rice and blend it separately in the same manner as the dahl to make a smooth paste.

Mix the two batters and the salt together in a large bowl. Cover the bowl with a breathable cloth, and put in a warm place where it won't be disturbed. Let the batter ferment for 12 to 15 hours, or longer, until the batter appears to have doubled in size and bubbles appear. Place a cookie sheet or cloth underneath in case the mixture overflows during the fermentation process.

Coat the molds of the idlis steamer with grease or cooking spray. Pour the batter into the molds, filling each two-thirds full, leaving room for it to rise. Put just enough water in the bottom of the steamer before putting the molds in to steam. Alternatively, pour the batter into the greased cups of an egg poacher. Steam for 10 to 12 minutes in the idlis steamer or egg poacher.

Remove the molds from the steamer or poacher, and allow to rest for 2 minutes before removing the idlis from the molds. Repeat until all the batter is used. Serve the hot idlis with coconut chutney, sambhar, or rasam.

Any remaining batter can be stored in the refrigerator for 4 days, though it's easier to cook the idlis, store them, and reheat. This batter is versatile and can be used for dosas as well.

**Makes 18 to 20; serves 8 to 10.**

# Rasam  रसम

Every time I visit my friend Rathna's house, I request that she make her special rasam. Rasam is a very thin soup with a tamarind or tomato base. It is a comfort food for me when I have a cold. It accompanies idlis and dosas. It can also be served with rice and yogurt or just as a light evening meal.

10 cups water

1 can (16 ounces) crushed tomatoes

3 tablespoons rasam powder (MTR brand, available in Indian grocery stores)

2 tablespoons tomato paste

1 2-inch piece of jaggery or 1 teaspoon monk fruit sweetener

½ teaspoon ground black pepper

1 tablespoon salt

1 teaspoon turmeric powder

**Tempering ingredients (place each in separate small bowls)**

¼ cup ghee or sunflower oil

½ teaspoon black mustard seeds

¼ teaspoon fenugreek seeds (methi)

8–10 curry leaves

⅛ teaspoon hing

1 red chili powder (optional)

Cilantro leaves

In a large pot, bring the water to a boil and add the tomatoes. Add the rasam powder, tomato paste, jaggery or monk fruit sweetener, black pepper, salt, and turmeric.

*Tempering the ingredients:* Heat a small saucepan on high. When the pan is hot, add the ghee, then immediately add the black mustard seeds, fenugreek seeds, and curry leaves. Once the seeds start to pop, add the hing and take the saucepan off the stove. Wait for 30 seconds, then add the spices to the tomato mixture in the pot. Add red chili powder and simmer for 3 to 5 minutes, or until piping hot. Mix well.

Garnish with cilantro and enjoy it like a soup on a cold winter day.

**Serves 6 to 8.**

# Sambhar सांभार

Sambhar is tridoshic (benefiting all body types). Sambhar can be served on its own as a comforting soup during the winter months to warm your belly. It is a wonderful accompaniment with dosas, idlis, rice, and yogurt. An all-time favorite, sambhar is served from the cheapest roadside stop to the classiest hotel in India. If you don't have a pressure cooker, you can cook this dish in a Crock-Pot. MTR brand spices are available in Indian grocery stores.

2 cups toovar or split massoor dahl

11–12 cups water

2 cups 2-inch pieces zucchini

3 tablespoons Vangi Bhath spice mix

3 tablespoons sambhar powder

1 teaspoon turmeric powder

¼ cup ghee

2 cups small-diced onions

½ green bell pepper, chopped

1 can (16 ounces) petite diced tomatoes

2 tablespoons tomato paste

2 tablespoons salt

1 cup peas

2 teaspoons tamarind paste

Pinch of cinnamon powder

1 1-inch piece of jaggery or 1 teaspoon sugar

½ cup small-diced or thinly sliced radishes (white daikon)

**Tempering ingredients (place each in separate small bowls)**

2 tablespoons ghee

½ teaspoon black mustard seeds

8–10 curry leaves

2 whole dried red chilies

⅛ teaspoon hing (optional)

Wash the dahl thoroughly and add to a pressure cooker with 10 cups of the water. Add the zucchini, spice mix, sambhar powder, and turmeric and allow the contents to come to a boil without the lid. Once the water starts to boil, close the lid and cook for 5 to 6 minutes after it starts to whistle. Turn the heat off, take it off the stove, and allow the pressure cooker to calm down inside before opening.

In the meantime, heat a large 6-quart saucepan on high with ghee. Add the onions and sauté on medium-high for 10 to 12 minutes, or until translucent. Add the bell pepper and saute for another 3 minutes.

Add the tomatoes, tomato paste, salt, and peas and mix thoroughly.

Open the pressure cooker and add the dahl mixture to the tomato mixture in the saucepan. Mix the contents with an immersion blender into a smooth consistency. If you want it to be thinner, add 1 to 2 cups of water until it reaches your desired consistency.

Add the tamarind, cinnamon, jaggery, and radishes.

*Tempering the ingredients:* Heat a small skillet on medium-high, then add the ghee and heat until hot but not smoking. Add the mustard seeds and allow the seeds to pop. Then add the curry leaves, red chilies, and hing (if desired). When fragrant, immediately remove from the heat and stir into the mixture in the saucepan.

Serve and enjoy!

**Serves 6 to 8.**

# Potato Filling for Dosa आलू मसाला

This is a great vegetable side dish as well as a filling for dosas. I would even serve it with rotis. It can be served with rice and yogurt as a dish. After all, rice and yogurt make a perfect protein. Adding potato is just another bonus. With the lime, serrano chili, and curry leaves, this filling has a distinctly South Indian flavor.

5 medium russet potatoes, whole and unpeeled

10 cups water

**Tempering ingredients (place each in separate small bowls)**

3 tablespoons vegetable oil

½ teaspoon mustard seeds

10 curry leaves

⅛ teaspoon hing

3 cups small-diced onions

2 serrano chilies, diced small

1 teaspoon turmeric

1 tablespoon salt (or to taste)

1–2 tablespoons fresh-squeezed lemon or lime juice

In a large pot, boil the potatoes in the water, covered, for 30 minutes. Remove from the water and cool until the potatoes can be handled. Peel the potatoes by rubbing the skin off with your fingers. Skins should slide off easily. Discard the skins and cut the potatoes into 3- to 4-inch chunks.

*Tempering the ingredients:* Heat a large pan on medium-high, and add the oil. Add the mustard seeds and curry leaves. Once the seeds start to pop, add the hing.

Add the onions to the tempered ingredients and sauté for 10 to 12 minutes, until translucent.

Add the serrano chilies, potatoes, turmeric, and salt, and stir well. Add lemon or lime juice.

**Serves 8 to 10.**

# *Karam Podi* कारम पोडी

I love a tablespoon of this in a cup of yogurt as a snack—it's my version of a savory yogurt. I sometimes add rice to it. Nicknamed "gunpowder," karam podi is not for the meek. It is a very spicy dish good for winter months, although the spices can be added at your own discretion. Serve it alongside dosas, idlis, rice, or yogurt. You can dry fresh curry leaves in the microwave by cooking them for 8 to 10 minutes on high. Allow them to cool and grind with the rest of the ingredients. Alternatively, you can buy dried curry leaves from an Indian grocery store.

1 tablespoon ghee

1 cup mung dahl

½ cup split urad dahl (or white dahl; see Dahl Chart on page 12)

½ cup massoor dahl

15 dried red chilies

1 tablespoon tamarind powder

1 teaspoon sugar

½ cup dried curry leaves

4 tablespoons paprika

¾ teaspoon hing

Heat the ghee in a saucepan on medium-high, and add the mung dahl, urad dahl, massoor dahl, and chilies. Toast, stirring constantly, for 7 to 8 minutes, until the ghee is absorbed and the lentils are lightly browned. Allow it to cool for 10 minutes. Place in a coffee grinder, and grind to a powder. Pour into a small bowl and set aside.

Add the tamarind, sugar, curry leaves, paprika, and hing to the grinder, and grind to a powder. Add it to the bowl with the spices and mix thoroughly. Store in a glass jar with a lid for up to 2 months. Karam podi does not need to be refrigerated.

**Serves 20.**

# Chettinad Curry चेट्टिनाड करी

I cannot help but smile at the memory of the first time I tasted Chettinad curry. I was in the Karaikudi district known as Chettinad in the Indian state of Tamil Nadu. I got to explore beautiful limestone palaces with artisans who made lovely silver and wood carvings. What was amazing were the spice and nut trees bearing cardamom, black pepper, cinnamon, and cashews that grew all around me. The owner of the guesthouse where we stayed proudly made this dish, which incorporates all the wonderful spices of the region, and served it on a banana leaf.

## Spice mixture

2 teaspoons coriander seeds

1 teaspoon cumin seeds

2 whole dried red chilies, broken into pieces

6 whole cardamoms

2 teaspoons fennel seeds

6 cloves

3 cinnamon sticks (1-inch pieces)

2 tablespoons poppy seeds

1 teaspoon turmeric powder

¼ cup cashews

2 tablespoons salt (or to taste)

## Vegetable mixture

¼ cup ghee

1 cup diced onions

1 tablespoon freshly grated ginger

6 curry leaves

1 can (16 ounces) petite diced tomatoes

7 cups cauliflower florets

2 cups peas (shelled if fresh)

2 cups diced green beans

1 can (16 ounces) coconut milk

2 cups water

1 teaspoon red chili powder

*To make the spice mixture:* Heat a small saucepan on medium-high, and dry-roast the coriander, cumin, chilies, cardamoms, fennel, cloves, and cinnamon. Stir constantly, until you smell a pleasant aroma of heated spices. Take off the stove, and allow to cool for 10 minutes. Then place them in a coffee grinder, and grind to a smooth powder. Add the poppy seeds, turmeric, cashews, and salt, and grind again to a powder. Set the spice mixture aside.

*To make the vegetable mixture:* In a large 6-quart saucepan, heat the ghee on medium-high, and add the onions, sautéing for 10 to 12 minutes, until translucent. Add the ginger and curry leaves, and cook for another 2 minutes. Then add the tomatoes and cook for 8 minutes, until they break down. Stir every 2 minutes so they do not burn.

Add the cauliflower, peas, and green beans and stir for 10 minutes, until al dente or to your desired consistency. Stir in the spice mixture and then the coconut milk, water, and red chili powder. Heat, mixing well, for 7 minutes, until well incorporated.

Serve hot over rice, with chapattis or naan, or as a favorite side dish with meat, fish, or chicken.

**Serves 8.**

From Iran with love comes biryani, whose journey began in Persia and continued to India where it has become a delicacy. It has been delighting and satiating hunger cravings for centuries in every corner of India. The word *biryani* comes from the Persian word *birian*, which means "fried before cooking"; *birinj* means "rice" in Farsi. In short, it's an elaborate version of fried rice cooked over charcoal in an earthen pot for a couple of days over a low flame.

There is another interesting legend of the origin of biryani. Mumtaz Mahal, the queen of the Mughal king Shah Jahan—in whose memory the Taj Mahal was built—once visited the army barracks and found the soldiers were undernourished. Concerned, she requested the royal chef prepare an economical dish that provided balanced nutrition for them. A dish of rice, vegetables, meat, and spices was created, with all ingredients thrown in one large pot and cooked over a low flame. The king was so impressed with the sumptuous aroma emanating from the pot, he wanted his chef to make it for him. The royal chef further developed the dish by adding nuts, saffron, more spices, and golden raisins and layered it with meat and vegetables before presenting it to the king. A poor man's meal became a trophy dish from the Mughal Empire.

Biryani is a fragrant, aromatic, heartwarming meal that tantalizes all the senses in one flavorful dish. It is layers of rice, meat, vegetables, spices, and sometimes a gravy. Some make it vegetarian; others make it with lamb, goat, or chicken. The possibilities are endless—and different regions have their own variations of this popular dish:

- Calcutta biryani
- Kalyani biryani
- Malabar biryani
- Hyderabadi biryani
- Dindigul biryani
- Katchi biryani

I developed my own variation called Bina's Chicken Curry for Biryani (recipe on page 94), which is now our family favorite. I serve this dish with Fresh Mint Raita (recipe on page 99) and garnish with nuts and hard-boiled eggs. It's a fantastic one-dish dinner that can be made ahead of time for family get-togethers. The leftovers taste even better the next day. Make it, relish it, and enjoy every bite!

# Chapter 5

# Ethnic Specialties

Bina's Chicken Curry for Biryani    94

Biryani Rice    96

Vegetable Biryani    98

Raita for Biryani and Dhansak    99

Fresh Mint Raita    99

Raw Salad    102

Dhansak    103

Caramelized Rice    106

Potato Raita with Hot Mustard    107

Thandai Spiced Almond Milk    110

# Bina's Chicken Curry for Biryani मुर्ग करी

Whenever my children come to visit, the first thing they ask me to make is my chicken biryani because they love it and can't wait to eat it. My daughter always asks me to make a lot so that she can take some home with her. This curry sauce is versatile—it can stand alone, be added to vegetables, or be used to make an egg curry without the chicken. This dish can be prepared a day or two ahead of time, stored in the refrigerator, and reheated.

**Spice paste**

10 cloves garlic, minced (2 tablespoons)

2–3 serrano chilies, minced

3 tablespoons grated ginger

1 cup finely chopped mint leaves

1 cup finely chopped cilantro leaves

**Dry spice mixture**

3 bay leaves

½ teaspoon saffron

1 ½ tablespoons garam masala (or try Bina's Garam Masala)

1 ½ tablespoons roasted cumin powder (or try Bina's Roasted Cumin)

2 teaspoons turmeric powder

2 tablespoons tandoori masala powder

1 tablespoon salt

**Chicken curry**

3 tablespoons ghee

1–1 ½ tablespoons mustard oil

3 tablespoons sunflower oil

3 large onions, diced small (around 3 cups)

3 tablespoons Patak's mild or hot curry paste (see page 205)

1 can (16 ounces) diced tomatoes

1 whole red bell pepper, diced

4 pounds bone-in, skinless chicken legs, thighs, and breasts

2 cups water or chicken or vegetable broth

Biryani Rice (recipe on page 96)

6 hard-boiled eggs (see box on page 95), optional

*To make the spice paste:* Blend the garlic, serrano chilies, ginger, mint, and cilantro in a blender or food processor.

*To make the dry spice mixture:* Measure the bay leaves, saffron, garam masala, cumin, turmeric, masala powder, and salt into a bowl.

*continued on page 95*

*continued from page 94*

*To make the chicken curry:* Preheat the oven to 375 degrees.

Heat the ghee, mustard oil, and sunflower oil in a 10-quart ovenproof saucepan or Dutch oven on medium-high. When hot, add the onions and sauté for 12 to 14 minutes, until translucent but not brown.

Reduce the heat to medium-low. Add the spice paste and cook for 6 minutes. Add Patak's curry paste and mix well. Add the tomatoes and bell pepper and cook for 6 to 8 minutes. Add the chicken and coat well with the mixture. Stir in the dry spice mixture and the water or broth, and mix well.

Bake the chicken, covered, for 2 hours, or until done (the meat should easily come off the bone).

While the chicken is cooking, make the Biryani Rice. Cool the rice to room temperature.

In a 9 x 13-inch pan, sandwich the chicken curry between layers of the rice, like lasagna. First add a layer of rice at the bottom of the pan, then add a layer of chicken curry, then another layer of rice, and so on. Finish with a layer of rice.

Just before serving, peel and slice the eggs (if desired) and place on top of the rice. You can also top with Caramelized Onions (recipe on page 106).

**Serves 12.**

### How to Make Perfect Hard-Boiled Eggs

Place the eggs in a pot with enough water to cover the tops of the eggs. Turn the heat to high. As soon as the water starts to boil, cook for 12 minutes. Immediately immerse the eggs in ice water and allow them to cool for 10 minutes. Peel.

# Biryani Rice बिरयानी चावल

*Basmati* means "fragrant." A long, slender grain grown at the foot of the Himalayas, basmati was cultivated for centuries before being discovered by the West. There are many varieties, and 60 percent of them come from India. I like to use basmati because it holds its shape, and it is fragrant and beautiful.

½ cup golden raisins

½ cup slivered almonds

½ cup shelled pistachios

½ cup cashews

**Tempering ingredients (place each in separate small bowls)**

⅓ cup ghee or vegetable oil

1 teaspoon cumin seeds

4 cloves

3 cinnamon sticks (1 ½-inch pieces)

6 whole cardamom pods

3 cups uncooked white basmati rice, rinsed and drained

5 ½ cups water

½ teaspoon saffron

1 tablespoon salt

In a bowl, combine the raisins, almonds, pistachios, and cashews. Set aside.

*Tempering the ingredients:* Heat the ghee or oil in an 8-quart saucepan on medium-high. When hot, add the cumin seeds and cook until they pop. While they are popping, add the cloves, cinnamon sticks, and cardamom pods, and cook for 1 minute, or until fragrant.

Add the rice and mix until well-coated with the oil.

Add the raisin-nut mixture and cook for about 30 seconds. Add the water and bring to a boil. Stir in the saffron and salt, reduce the heat to medium, and simmer for 12 to 15 minutes, without stirring, until almost all the water is absorbed. Turn off the stove and cover for 10 minutes, allowing the rice to steam undisturbed. Do not lift the cover while steaming.

**Serves 12.**

# *Vegetable Biryani* सब्जी बिरयानी

**This is a vegetarian version of biryani.**

## Vegetables

1 cup chopped green beans

1 cup small-diced red bell peppers

1 cup small cauliflower florets

1 cup small-diced carrots

1 cup peas

## Spice mixtures

1 cup chopped cilantro

1 cup chopped mint leaves

1 tablespoon minced garlic

2 tablespoons grated ginger

1 serrano chili, cut in half

½ cup vegetable broth

½ teaspoon saffron

1 tablespoon garam masala (or try Bina's Garam Masala)

1 tablespoon salt

3 tablespoons ghee

1–1 ½ tablespoons mustard oil

3 tablespoons sunflower oil

2 ½ cups small-diced onions

1 bay leaf

2 tablespoons Patak's mild curry paste (see page 205)

1 tablespoon tandoori masala powder

1 can (16 ounces) crushed tomatoes

Biryani Rice (recipe on page 96)

*To prepare the vegetables:* In a large bowl, combine the green beans, bell pepper, cauliflower, carrots, and peas. Set aside.

*To make the spice mixtures:* Make a paste by blending the cilantro, mint, garlic, ginger, serrano chili, and broth in a blender or food processor. Set aside.

In a small bowl, combine the saffron, garam masala, and salt.

In a 10-quart ovenproof saucepan or Dutch oven, heat the ghee, mustard oil, and sunflower oil on medium-high. When hot, add the onions and sauté for 12 to 15 minutes, until translucent but not brown. Reduce the heat to medium-low, add the spice paste, and cook for 6 minutes, until the water is reduced. Add the bay leaf, Patak's curry paste, and tandoori masala powder, and mix well. Add the vegetables and mix well. Cook for 15 to 20 minutes, or until al dente.

Add the tomatoes and cook, stirring continuously, for 9 minutes until they break down. Stir in the saffron mixture.

Add a cup of water and continue cooking on medium-high for 20 minutes, stirring continuously. This dish can also be covered and baked in the oven at 375 degrees for 20 to 25 minutes.

When it's done cooking or baking, layer the vegetables and Biryani Rice in a 9 x 13-inch pan, like lasagna. Start with a layer of rice at the bottom of the pan, then add a layer of vegetables, then another layer of rice, and so on. Finish with a layer of rice on top.

Garnish with Caramelized Onions (see recipe on page 106).

Serve with a raita (see recipes on page 99) and Raw Salad (recipe on page 102).

**Serves 6.**

# Raita for Biryani and Dhansak  धानसाक रायता

This is a perfect accompaniment for Biryani (recipes on pages 94, 96 and 98) or Dhansak (recipe on page 103).

5 cups plain yogurt

1 tablespoon small-diced serrano chilies

1 cup chopped green onions

1 cup chopped cilantro leaves

1 tablespoon salt

In a large bowl, whisk the yogurt until smooth. Add the serrano chilies, green onions, and cilantro, and mix well. Stir in the salt.

**Serves 6 to 8.**

# Fresh Mint Raita  फुदीना रायता

This dish complements almost any meal—lamb, chicken, vegetables, lentils, parathas—and is refreshing on a hot summer's day. It is cooling for spicy dishes and healthy at any time.

3 cups plain yogurt

1 cup chopped mint leaves

½ tablespoon salt (or to taste)

½ teaspoon chaat masala (or try Bina's Bombay Masala Blend)

In a medium bowl, mix the yogurt and mint. Add the salt and masala and mix well. Chill until cold, and then serve.

**Serves 6 to 8.**

You can buy yogurt at the store, but you might want to make your own. See recipe on page 115.

# Raw Salad सलाद

This refreshing salad features raw, crunchy vegetables that pair especially well with biryani (recipes on pages 94 and 98) and Dhansak (recipe on page 103). Try serving it with any other menu. Sumac, a souring agent, makes the salad beautiful with its red color.

½ medium white onion, sliced

½ medium red onion, sliced

10 small red radishes, sliced

1 large white radish (daikon), sliced

2 carrots, sliced

1 teaspoon sumac

½ teaspoon salt

3 limes, cut into wedges

Place the onions, radishes, and carrots in a large bowl. Sprinkle with the sumac, salt, and lime juice, and mix well.

**Serves 6 to 8.**

# *Dhansak* धानसाक

This unique dish is a jewel of the Parsis and is renowned all over India. When the Parsis left Iran and settled in Gujarat, they adapted their ancestral dish to the ingredients—vegetables, legumes, aromatics, herbs, and spices—available in their new home. The name rightly suggests the nature of the dish: *dhan* refers to abundant wealth, and *sak* refers to vegetables. Dhansak is a healthy comfort food and is a substantial dish, enjoyed by families for Sunday brunch. Although this recipe is vegetarian, feel free to adapt and include a protein of your choice, such as lamb or mutton. It can also be served with a chicken kebab as an accompaniment and garnished with fried caramelized onions.

## Dahl and vegetables

1 cup toovar dahl

2 tablespoons split urad dahl (or white dahl; see Dahl Chart on page 12)

2 tablespoons mung dahl

2 tablespoons massoor dahl

1 medium potato, peeled and quartered

½ small eggplant, quartered

2 tomatoes, quartered

1 medium yellow squash, cut into chunks

1 medium zucchini, cut into chunks

7 green onions with tops, cut into 1-inch pieces

6 ounces frozen fenugreek (methi) leaves or 1 bunch fresh leaves

5 cups water

## Spice mixtures*

2 serrano chilies

10 large garlic cloves

2-inch piece of ginger

1 large bunch cilantro leaves

¼ cup water

1 tablespoon red chili powder

4 cinnamon sticks, or 2 teaspoons cinnamon powder

3 cloves, or ¼ teaspoon ground

5 black peppercorns, or ½ teaspoon ground

5 green cardamom pods, or ¾ teaspoon ground

1 ½ tablespoons cumin seeds, or 1 ¾ tablespoons ground

5 tablespoons ghee

2 medium red or white onions, finely chopped

3 tablespoons tamarind paste

2 tablespoons salt

1 teaspoon garam masala (or try Bina's Garam Masala)

2 teaspoons turmeric powder

3 tablespoons dhansak masala (optional—available in ethnic Indian stores)

*To make the dahl and vegetables:* Wash the toovar dahl, urad dahl, mung dahl, and massoor dahl in warm water, and then rinse and drain. Note: You can use any or all of these dahls, but use these amounts.

In a large bowl, place the potato, eggplant, tomatoes, squash, zucchini, green onions, and fenugreek. Add the dahl mixture and combine.

Place the vegetable-dahl mixture and the water in an Instant Pot or pressure cooker. If using an Instant Pot, follow instructions; it shouldn't take more than 30 minutes. If using a pressure cooker, cook on medium-high until the pressure cooker whistles. Turn the heat off, and allow the pressure to dissipate before opening it. After opening the pressure cooker without forcing, use an immersion blender to blend the mixture together. If using an Instant Pot, use the immersion blender to blend the mixture together.

*To make the spice mixtures:* In a blender, place the serrano chilies, garlic, ginger, cilantro, and water. Blend to make a smooth paste. Set aside.

In a coffee grinder, add the red chili powder, cinnamon sticks, cloves, whole peppercorns, cardamom pods, and cumin seeds. Grind to a smooth powder. If using powdered spices, mix together in a small bowl. Set aside.

In a 4-quart saucepan, heat the ghee on medium-high. Once hot, add the onions and sauté for 12 to 15 minutes, or until translucent but not browned. Stir in both spice mixtures and cook for 4 minutes, or until the liquid is absorbed. Add the vegetable-dahl mixture and combine.

Stir in the tamarind, salt, garam masala, turmeric, and dhansak masala (if desired). Simmer on medium-low, stirring constantly, for 9 to 10 minutes, until hot.

Serve warm with Caramelized Rice (recipe on page 106), Raw Salad (recipe on page 102), or Potato Raita with Hot Mustard (recipe on page 107).

**Serves 12.**

* *If you would rather not use whole spices, please see the Whole Spice Conversion Chart on page 5.*

# Caramelized Rice प्याज चावल

This mouthwatering dish is perfect with **Dhansak (recipe on page 103)**, but it's sumptuous served with any of your meat or vegetable recipes as a side dish or on its own with yogurt. **Caramelizing the onions adds the brown color to the rice and enhances the flavor.**

5 tablespoons ghee

2 onions, finely chopped

2 cinnamon sticks

2 green cardamom pods

2 cloves

1 ½ tablespoons sugar

3 cups uncooked basmati rice, washed and drained

6 cups water

1 teaspoon salt

In a 4-quart saucepan, heat the ghee on medium-high. Fry the onions, cinnamon, cardamom, cloves, and sugar on high, stirring constantly, until the onions turn a dark brown color but are not burnt.

Add the rice and coat with the mixture. Add the water and salt and bring to a boil on medium-high. Cook, uncovered, for 15 to 20 minutes, until the liquid is almost absorbed. Do not stir. Cover and turn off the stove, to allow steam to finish the rice. Do not uncover or disturb for 10 minutes.

Allow the rice to come to room temperature before serving. If you scoop the rice out too soon when it's still hot, the grains can break.

**Serves 12.**

## Caramelized Onions

**These can be used as a garnish for dhansak or biriyanis, on steak, or with any of your favorite dishes. They're delicious!**

4 tablespoons ghee (or more if needed)
2 tablespoons vegetable oil
3 pounds yellow onions, thinly sliced

In a large skillet, heat the ghee and oil on medium-high. Add the onions, stirring well to coat, and cook on high, stirring constantly, for 20 to 25 minutes, or until well browned and caramelized. (There's a fine line between caramelized and burnt!)

Use a slotted spoon to remove the onions and place them on paper towels to drain. As they cool, they will become crisp.

# Potato Raita with Hot Mustard  आलू रायता

**Tired of the same old potato salad? Try this exotic version instead. This makes a great side dish for many entrees, vegetables, and breads. Or try it in place of mashed potatoes.**

3 medium potatoes

5 cups plain yogurt

1 tablespoon salt

3 tablespoons hot mustard powder

**Tempering ingredients (place each in separate small bowls)**

1 tablespoon vegetable oil

½ teaspoon mustard seeds

2 whole dried red chilies

6–8 curry leaves

Put the potatoes in a 4-quart saucepan with a lid. Cover with water, and boil for 20 to 25 minutes, or until easily pierced with a knife. Drain immediately and submerge in cold water. Peel the skin by rubbing it off with your fingers, and discard. Cut the potatoes into large chunks.

Meanwhile, mix the yogurt, salt, and mustard powder. Fold in the warm potatoes and mix well. Set aside.

*Tempering the ingredients:* In a small saucepan, heat the oil on medium-high. When it's hot, add the mustard seeds, red chilies, and curry leaves (the mustard seeds will make a spluttering noise). Take the pan off the stove immediately and pour the spices over the potatoes. Mix well.

Chill until cold and then serve.

**Serves 6 to 8.**

*Whole milk will bring the richest flavor, but you can try combinations of almond or cashew milk, or even water.

# Thandai Spiced Almond Milk  ठंडाई

A power drink, thandai spiced milk is perfect for a hot day or when eating spicy food. It's served at Indian parties on festival days and outside Hindu temples with bhang. Be careful of bhang—it is the stem of the marijuana plant and can cause intoxication.

¼ cup golden raisins

½ cup warm water (for the raisins)

2 tablespoons fennel seeds

2 teaspoons poppy seeds

¾ teaspoon black peppercorns

½ teaspoon green cardamom seeds

3 cups water (for the almonds)

½ cup raw unsalted almonds

1 teaspoon saffron, plus a few strands for garnish

4 tablespoons gulkand (rose petal jam)

7 cups whole milk*

In a small bowl, cover the raisins with the warm water and let soak. Set aside.

In a coffee grinder, grind the fennel seeds, poppy seeds, peppercorns, and cardamom seeds to a powder. Set aside.

Add the water to a small pot and bring to a boil. Add the almonds and boil for exactly 1 minute. Don't boil any longer than that or the almonds will begin to "cook" and soften. Drain the almonds and immediately rinse with cold water to stop the cooking process. While still warm, squeeze the almonds gently to loosen the skins. The almond should slip right out of its skin. Discard the skins. (See box below.)

Place the raisins, almonds, ground spice blend, saffron, gulkand, and milk in a blender and blend well. Refrigerate for at least 6 hours or, for best taste, overnight. The saffron will lend a golden color.

To serve, strain and pour into a 2-ounce glass with a few strands of saffron as garnish. Serve chilled.

**Serves 6 to 8.**

*Note: If you don't have time for blanching, you can find blanched and skinned almonds in the frozen food section of your grocery store.*

Blanching is the term for plunging ingredients in boiling water for a very limited time and then submerging them in either iced or cold water to stop the cooking process. Blanching is often used to loosen skin from vegetables, fruit, or nuts.

If you're feeling sluggish or unwell, it might be time to press the reset button with a detox. No need to panic—it is possible to enjoy delicious and satisfying meals while removing toxins from your body. This menu will help you do this. A detox will energize, rejuvenate, and rev up your metabolism. The best time to do one is when the seasons change.

A good detox should not be focused on deprivation. You can eliminate toxins from your body without starving yourself. You should eat three meals a day with fresh, natural ingredients and avoid processed food and overeating. One of the key things to understand is your body constitution or prakriti—your unique biological blueprint—which will help you make food choices based on an awareness of what works best for you (see "About Ayurveda" on page v). Our bodies are always talking to us … are you listening?

Ayurveda teaches that to eat is human, but to digest is divine. One emphasis in Ayurveda is on the digestive metabolic fire, agni. Agni is our ability to metabolize the food we eat, to provide proper nutrition and cellular intelligence to our body so that it functions at its optimum. When this digestive metabolic fire is impaired, then the toxins produced by the undigested food create havoc in our body, causing clogging and an overall decline in health. We end up with symptoms such as feeling sluggish and heavy or having aching joints and muscles, brain fog, fatigue, headaches, allergies, gas, arthritis, diseases, or poor elimination. When we ignore this, we are ignoring our system's internal warning bells and whistles.

My menu is designed to help you enjoy a detox. You'll find recipes that the body can assimilate and absorb easily and that also aid the elimination and cleansing process. This will bring back vitality and life force—ojas—in your system.

Khitchdi is an especially effective food for cleansing because it is a perfect protein and is tasty. Eat foods that are easy for the body to process and digest, such as soups with seasonal vegetables, or plain rice and yogurt. These will allow your agni to jump-start your metabolism. When you are ready to replenish and rebuild your immune system, try the Light Dinner Menu options starting on page 132.

# Chapter 6

# Ayurveda Menu

Khitchdi                                     114
Yogurt                                       115
Chaash                                       116
Coconut Kadhi                                118
Green Power Drink                            119
Delightful Cashew Coconut Curry  120
Mung Dahl                                    121
Gujarati Kadhi                               122
Eggplant Raita                               123
Khao Suey                                    126
Trevti Dahl                                  128

# *Khitchdi* खिचड़ी

The first meal I look forward to after a long trip of indulgent eating is a simple, comforting, and nourishing bowl of khitchdi, to give my tummy a rest. It's so easy to digest that it is also a wholesome food for newborn babies, the elderly, and the sick. For a cleanse or a detox, this is a perfectly balanced meal that can be eaten for several days. This one-pot dish is made with rice, dahl, and ghee—a delicious Indian risotto. Every region in India has different lentils and grains for making khitchdi, such as massoor dahl, toovar dahl, and buckwheat. If you are eating it every day, vary it by using different seasonal vegetables so you do not get bored!

1 ½ cups split mung dahl with husks

1 ½ cups rice (brown and white mixed)

10–12 cups water

1 cinnamon stick

10 black peppercorns

1 teaspoon turmeric powder

1 tablespoon grated ginger

1 ½ tablespoons salt (or to taste)

1 cup chopped cauliflower

1 potato, peeled and diced small

1 cup diced carrots or baby carrots

**Tempering ingredients (place each in separate small bowls)**

4 tablespoons ghee

1 teaspoon cumin seeds

½ teaspoon red chili powder

½ teaspoon garam masala (or try Bina's Garam Masala)

Wash the split mung dahl and rice, and drain.

In a deep 4-quart saucepan, add 8 cups of the water, the dahl, rice, cinnamon stick, peppercorns, turmeric, ginger, and salt. Heat on medium-high until it boils, then reduce the heat to medium-low and add the cauliflower, potato, and carrots. Simmer, covered, for 20 to 25 minutes, stirring regularly until porridge consistency is reached. Add the remaining 2–4 cups water as needed to create the desired consistency. Cook for another 10 minutes.

*Tempering the ingredients:* In a small skillet, heat the ghee on high and add the cumin seeds. Once the seeds start to pop, remove the skillet from the stove. Add the red chili powder and garam masala.

Immediately add the tempered ingredients to the khitchdi, and mix well. Serve hot.

**Serves 6.**

# Yogurt  दही

Yogurt has been one of my two comfort foods since my early years in India and was a staple of every meal. It is not rocket science to make your own. Yogurt is milk fermented with a live yogurt culture and, ironically, is far easier to digest and assimilate than milk. Yogurt is packed with protein, calcium, and other vitamins and minerals, and has a powerhouse of essential active probiotic cultures that are good for your digestive track. Store-bought yogurt, which has been refrigerated and sitting on the shelf for an extended period of time, has less active beneficial bacteria than homemade yogurt. Make plain yogurt to start; you can add your own flavors after it is done. Once it is made, save 5 to 6 tablespoons as a starter for your next batch.

½ gallon whole milk

3 tablespoons plain organic yogurt (I like Dannon, Mountain High, Chobani, or Stonyfield, which have good, live, active bacteria in them)

Place the milk in a glass container. Put it in the microwave, and heat for 16 to 17 minutes to boiling, until a film forms on the top. Remove and let cool to 125 degrees (use a candy thermometer). It has to be 125 degrees for the next step.

Add the yogurt and mix well.

Pour the mixture into a container with a lid and cover. Place it in a location at room temperature where the mixture will not be disturbed for 8 to 10 hours. An unheated oven can be a safe place to allow the yogurt to incubate overnight. Check it after 8 hours to see if it is set. It will be less liquid and more like a thick custard or pudding.

Once the yogurt is set, you can store it in the refrigerator for up to 10 days.

Note: Seasonal temperatures can affect the yogurt-making process. If you are making yogurt on a hot summer day, use 1 teaspoon less culture than the recipe calls for. On cold winter days, you may use 1 teaspoon more culture. If you add too much culture, the yogurt will come out overly sour.

**Makes 2 quarts.**

*Ayurveda recognizes yogurt as the only fermented food that is Sattvic. Sattvic foods are fresh, juicy, light, nourishing, and tasty, and thus give necessary energy to the body and help achieve balance. It has a sour taste that balances vata, but should be used in smaller amounts by people who are pitta and kapha.*

## *Chaash (Buttermilk)*

Enjoy a glass of delicious homemade buttermilk, or chaash, to aid with digestion and absorption. This delight is found in many cultures and many parts of the world, including the Middle East, Eastern Europe, and Asia. Once you taste homemade buttermilk, you will never buy it from the supermarket again.

To make two glasses of this refreshing, cooling drink, blend until frothy:

⅛ teaspoon roasted cumin powder
(or try Bina's Roasted Cumin)
1 teaspoon sea salt
1 cup plain yogurt
3 cups water

Garnish with mint leaves.

Yogurt and rice (my other comfort food) are a perfect protein combination. In a pinch, simply combine:

1 cup cooked basmati rice
1 ½ cups yogurt
or plain organic yogurt
Salt (to taste)

Garnish with ground black pepper.

# Coconut Kadhi नारियल कढ़ी

This is a dairy-free version of Gujarati Kadhi (recipe on page 122). Try serving it with steamed spiced vegetables, rice, or khitchdi. It can even be a soup. It is delightful!

2 cups coconut yogurt

5 cups water

4 tablespoons besan (chickpea flour)

1 tablespoon salt

**Tempering ingredients (place each in separate small bowls)**

3 tablespoons ghee

1 teaspoon cumin seeds

1 serrano chili, sliced

3–4 slices of ginger

1 cinnamon stick

10 curry leaves

1 white radish, thinly sliced

10 leaves mint or cilantro, plus extra for garnish

In a 4-quart saucepan, mix the yogurt, water, besan, and salt, and stir well to remove all lumps. Heat on high, stirring constantly to thicken the soup and keep it from separating. Once it thickens, reduce the heat to medium-low and allow to simmer.

*Tempering the ingredients:* In a small skillet, heat the ghee on high. When it is hot, add the cumin seeds. When the seeds start to pop, add the serrano chili, ginger, cinnamon, and curry leaves.

Immediately pour the tempered ingredients over the yogurt mixture and blend well. Add the radish and mint and bring to a boil. Simmer for 5 to 7 minutes.

Garnish with mint or cilantro and serve hot.

**Serves 6 to 8.**

# Green Power Drink with Kale and Cucumber ग्रीन पावर ड्रिंक

Drink your veggies every day! Get that internal radiance and glow with this delicious drink and alkalize yourself to feel great. This Ayurvedic superfood drink boosts your immune system and helps build healthy bones and a healthy, happy heart. Green vegetables like kale, spinach, collard greens, mint, and cilantro are nutritional powerhouses that increase energy and improve digestion. Great for a detox!

¾ cup kale, rough stems removed, or baby spinach

1 cup mint leaves

1 cup cilantro leaves

1 cup peeled and chopped English cucumber

1 cup chopped zucchini

1 tablespoon grated ginger

½ teaspoon ground black pepper

½ teaspoon roasted cumin powder (or try Bina's Roasted Cumin)

5 tablespoons lime juice (or to taste)

6 cups water

2 cups ice

Add all the ingredients to a high-speed blender and blend until liquefied. Serve chilled.

The ingredients may separate if the drink sits for a few minutes. Stir with a spoon to incorporate all ingredients before serving.

**Serves 6.**

# Delightful Cashew Coconut Curry काजू नारियल करी

This is a fantastic, complex combination of sweet and spicy flavors. While the vegetables are steaming, all the spices can be roasted. It is a quick, easy, and ridiculously tasty dish that is hard to resist. You will want to lick your plate clean!

1 cup diced carrots

1 green bell pepper, chopped

1 small cauliflower head, cut into small florets

2 tablespoons water

**Dry-roasted spices**

3 tablespoons coriander seeds

1 tablespoon cumin seeds

5–6 dried red chilies (optional)

4 cinnamon sticks

1 teaspoon poppy seeds

1 tablespoon salt

2 tablespoons paprika

1 cup unsalted raw cashews

¼ cup ghee or vegetable oil

6 cloves garlic, minced

1 large onion, diced small

1½ cups peas

2 tablespoons tomato paste

1 can (16 ounces) unsweetened coconut milk

½ cup water

Place the carrots, bell pepper, and cauliflower in a bowl with the water, cover with plastic wrap, and steam in the microwave on high for 5 minutes, until tender.

*To dry-roast the spices:* Meanwhile, heat a small saucepan on medium-high and add the coriander seeds, cumin seeds, chilies (if desired), cinnamon, and poppy seeds. Heat for 3 minutes, until warm and fragrance is released. Do not overcook. Allow the spices to cool, then place them in a coffee grinder and grind to a powder.

Add the salt, paprika, and cashews and grind to a powder.

In a 6-quart saucepan, heat the ghee or oil on medium-high and add the garlic and onions. Sauté for 12 minutes, or until the onions become translucent. Add the spices, steamed vegetables, and peas and mix well. Stir in the tomato paste, coconut milk, and water. When the mixture is blended, allow to bubble and then serve hot.

**Serves 8.**

# Mung Dahl मुंग दाल

The unassuming yellow split mung bean can offer a warm, nourishing feeling of joy to the tummy. This is a bowlful of contentment and relief to a bloated and uncomfortable belly. This little lentil helps tone digestive organs with its astringent taste. The bean's fiber helps cleanse the colon by purging the toxins and mucus that may be lodged in your gut. It is no surprise that these tasty lentils have gained popularity in the United States.

2 cups split mung beans

¼ cup chana dahl

2 tablespoons peeled and grated ginger

¼ teaspoon fenugreek seeds (methi), optional

1 medium zucchini, diced

1 teaspoon turmeric powder

1 tablespoon salt

6 cups water

3 tablespoons ground coriander

2 teaspoons red chili powder

2 tablespoons lemon juice

**Tempering ingredients (place each in separate small bowls)**

4 tablespoons ghee

1 teaspoon cumin seeds

1 serrano chili, sliced

10 curry leaves

Pinch of hing (optional)

Chopped cilantro leaves

Add the mung beans, chana dahl, ginger, fenugreek (if desired), zucchini, turmeric, salt, and water to a pressure cooker (see box below). Turn the heat on high and cook for 6 to 7 minutes, until the cooker whistles. Turn the heat off, but keep it on the stove to continue cooking with residual heat for another 20 to 30 minutes. Be patient and wait for the pressure to be released from the pressure cooker. It should slide open effortlessly.

After opening the pressure cooker, use an immersion blender to blend the dahl mixture. Then add the coriander, red chili powder, and lemon juice, and mix well.

*Tempering the ingredients:* In a small skillet, heat the ghee on high. Add the cumin seeds and serrano chili. When the seeds start to pop, add the curry leaves and hing (if desired). Immediately add the tempered spices to the dahl and mix well.

Dahl tends to thicken as it cools. If the dahl is too thick, add water to create your desired consistency.

Garnish with cilantro and serve hot.

**Serves 6 to 8.**

> *The dahl can be cooked on the stove if a pressure cooker is not available. You will need to soak the beans overnight and boil on the stove for 1½ to 2 hours with constant stirring. Once that is done, use an immersion blender to blend the dahl mixture. Then follow the rest of the recipe instructions.*

# Gujarati Kadhi गुजराती कढ़ी

**Yogurt, water, and besan are the primary ingredients of this mouthwatering treat, which has a sweet and sour taste. It can be eaten with khitchdi and rice, and pairs well with vegetables. I eat it like soup sometimes when I want a light dinner. For a dairy-free option, make the Coconut Kadhi (recipe on page 118).**

2 cups Yogurt (recipe on page 115) or plain organic yogurt

5 cups water

4 tablespoons besan (chickpea flour)

1 tablespoon salt

**Tempering ingredients (place each in separate small bowls)**

3 tablespoons ghee

1 teaspoon cumin seeds

1 serrano chili, sliced

3–4 slices of ginger

1 cinnamon stick

10 curry leaves

4 thin slices white radish

10 leaves mint or cilantro, plus extra for garnish

In a 4-quart saucepan, mix the yogurt, water, besan, and salt, and stir well to remove all lumps. Heat on high, stirring constantly to thicken the soup and keep it from separating. Once it thickens, reduce the heat to medium-low and allow to simmer.

*Tempering the ingredients:* In a small skillet, heat the ghee on high. When it is hot, add the cumin seeds. When the seeds start to pop, add the serrano chili, ginger, cinnamon, and curry leaves.

Pour the tempered ingredients over the yogurt mixture and blend well. Add the radish and mint and bring to a boil, then simmer for 5 to 7 minutes.

Garnish with mint or cilantro and serve hot.

**Serves 6 to 8.**

*This dish goes well with Khitchdi (recipe on page 114).*

# Eggplant Raita  बैंगन रायता

Eggplant dishes take a starring role at an Indian meal. Eggplant has a delicious smoky flavor after being roasted and charred, and in India, that flavor comes from it being cooked on the embers of charcoal. I love this recipe. My friend Diana does not like eggplant, but she loved this when I made it for her. This simple dish can be made ahead of time and stored in the refrigerator for 3 to 4 days and eaten as a salad.

2 large eggplants

½ cup small-diced onions

2 serrano chilies, finely minced (optional)

1 teaspoon roasted cumin powder (or try Bina's Roasted Cumin)

1 tablespoon salt (or to taste)

4 cups plain yogurt

5 tablespoons finely chopped cilantro leaves

Preheat the oven to 450 degrees. Place the eggplants on a baking sheet and make four slits in each one, to keep them from bursting in the oven. Roast for 45 minutes, or until easily pierced by a fork. Remove and allow to cool.

Meanwhile, place the onions, serrano chilies (if desired), cumin, salt, and yogurt in a large bowl.

When the eggplants are cool, use a spoon to remove the pulp from the skin, discarding the skin. Add the pulp to the onion-yogurt mixture.

Garnish with the cilantro and serve cold.

**Serves 8.**

# Khao Suey खाओ सूई

A coconut soup served like a ramen bowl, Khao Suey (pronounced "how sway") is an explosion of flavors. It is my favorite soup and a great party dish often served at Indian weddings. Once all the prep work is done, it takes 10 minutes to put the dish together. This recipe is an adaptation of a Myanmar (Burmese) dish. I like it as a vegetarian dish, but you can add your favorite cooked protein—shrimp, chicken, and paneer go well. It is gluten-free, dairy-free, and soy-free.

## Dry-roasted spices

1 teaspoon coriander seeds

1 teaspoon cumin seeds

2 cloves

2 cinnamon sticks

3–4 dried red chilies

3 teaspoons white poppy seeds (khus-khus)

## Garnish options

1 cup shredded carrots (fresh or frozen)

1 cup chopped green beans (fresh or frozen)

¼ cup chopped cilantro leaves

4 green onions, diced

¼ cup crushed roasted peanuts (salted or unsalted)

1 small onion, sliced and caramelized (see "Caramelized Onions" box on page 106)

¼ cup lime juice

## Soup

1 pound rice noodles

3 tablespoons coconut oil

1 small onion, finely diced

6 cloves garlic, thinly sliced

2 tomatoes, finely diced

9 cups coconut milk (canned) or coconut powder (follow instructions)

*To make the dry-roasted spices:* Place the coriander, cumin, cloves, cinnamon, chilies, and poppy seeds in a saucepan on medium heat. Roast for 2 to 3 minutes, or until fragrant, shaking the skillet constantly so they do not burn. Let cool completely, then blend into a powder with a mortar and pestle or coffee grinder. Set aside. (This can be done days ahead of time and stored for up to two months. You might want to double this spice blend recipe and keep it for the future.)

*To make the garnish options:* Place the carrots, green beans, cilantro, green onions, peanuts, caramelized onions, and lime juice in separate bowls.

*continued on page 127*

*continued from page 126*

*To make the soup:* Boil the rice noodles following package directions, then drain and rinse. Store in cool water until needed.

Heat the oil in a pot on medium-high. Sauté the onions for 10 to 12 minutes, until translucent. Add the garlic and sauté until golden. Stir in the tomatoes and cook for 8 minutes, until soft. Add the dry-roasted spices, blending well, and then the coconut milk. Remove from the heat once tiny bubbles begin to form around the edges.

To assemble, place ½ cup boiled noodles in a bowl, ladle 1 ½ cups of the soup, and serve. Allow guests to garnish the soup as they desire.

**Serves 6.**

# Trevti Dahl (Three Mixed Dahls) लेवटी दाल

Trevti Dahl is a healthy, light option for an evening meal. You can drink it as a soup or pour it over rice. You can also add fresh greens, like spinach, to enhance the dish. This will nourish and fill you up while on a detox or cleanse.

1 ½ cups split mung dahl

¼ cup split urad dahl (or white dahl; see Dahl Chart on page 112)

¼ cup chana dahl

8 cups water (divided)

1 tablespoon salt

1 teaspoon turmeric powder

1 tablespoon grated ginger

**Tempering ingredients (place each in separate small bowls)**

2 tablespoons ghee

1 teaspoon cumin seeds

1 serrano chili, sliced

12 curry leaves

Pinch of hing (optional)

2 tablespoons fresh lime juice

2 tablespoons chopped cilantro leaves

Rinse and drain the mung dahl, urad dahl, and chana dahl.

Add the dahls, 6 cups of the water, the salt, turmeric, and ginger to a pressure cooker (see box below). Cook on medium-high until the cooker whistles. Turn the heat off, but leave it on the stove to continue cooking with residual heat for another 20 to 30 minutes. Be patient and wait for the pressure to be released from the pressure cooker. It should slide open effortlessly. Use an immersion blender to blend the dahl mixture.

*Tempering the ingredients:* In a small skillet, heat the ghee on medium-high. Once the oil is hot, add the cumin seeds. When the seeds start to pop, add the serrano chili, curry leaves, and hing (if desired). Immediately remove from the heat.

Add the tempered spices to the dahl. Add the remaining 2 cups water and the lime juice. Mix well. Allow to simmer on medium-low for 6 to 8 minutes, until it boils. Garnish with the cilantro, and then serve.

**Serves 6 to 8.**

> *The dahl can be cooked in a slow cooker if a pressure cooker is not available. Place the dahls, water, salt, turmeric, and ginger in the slow cooker on high for 3 hours. Then complete the recipe following the directions above.*

There are times that our internal cleansing system has been compromised or is not operating at its optimal strength to convert food into nutrition. It is at these times that a lighter menu is recommended, to allow the body to gradually regain balance and strength to increase the ability for digestive fire (agni). This menu is preferred when recuperating from a fever, cold, flu, or upset stomach because it digests easily and quickly. Children and babies often eat lighter meals, and this diet is recommended for them as well as for women going through their monthly (or moon) cycle.

Homemade Indian food is very light, healthy, and nutritious. Spices and aromatics such as coriander, cumin, turmeric, ginger, and garlic add medicinal benefits without increasing calories. Indian food is quite amazing, providing benefits to the mind, emotions, body, and spirit.

Indian restaurant food tends to be heavier since it is cooked with cream or malai. It is important to choose the correct things on the menu. Chicken tikkas, kebabs, and tandoori specialties that are grilled are excellent choices. A bowl of curry, spinach saag, eggplant, yogurt raita, butternut squash, and rice dahl all provide a satisfying meal with naan and roti. Fried things do add the calories, but they can be a treat now and then.

In this section, I have provided some recipes for healthy light options. The single lightest diet food, according to Ayurveda, is split mung beans (see Dahl Chart on page 12), which balances all doshas. The Ayurveda Menu (Chapter 6) includes several recipes with mung dahl, including Khitchdi (page 114), an excellent one-dish meal for people on a light diet. Rekindle your agni and restore your metabolism with this healing menu.

# Chapter 7

# Light Dinner Menu

| | |
|---|---|
| Butternut Squash | 132 |
| Golden Milk Elixir | 133 |
| Sprouted Mung Salad and Dressing | 136 |
| Fragrant Saffron Basmati Rice | 137 |
| Massoor Dahl with Spinach | 140 |
| Macchi | 141 |
| Mango Pomegranate Salad | 144 |
| Coconut Burfi | 145 |

# Butternut Squash बटरनट स्क्वाश

Butternut squash is a winter squash and is a great substitute for white potatoes since it has fewer calories and more nutrients. It has more potassium than a banana and provides beta-carotene and vitamin C. And it has a natural, sweet flavor without sugar. I have created this recipe with love. Sweet potatoes or yams can be substituted for the squash.

1 teaspoon turmeric powder

1 tablespoon salt

3 tablespoons ground coriander

1 tablespoon red chili powder

**Tempering ingredients (place each in separate small bowls)**

⅓ cup vegetable oil

1 teaspoon black mustard seeds

Pinch of hing (optional)

1 large butternut squash, peeled, seeded, and cut into 1 ½-inch cubes (12 cups)

2 tablespoons lime juice

4 tablespoons chopped cilantro leaves

Mix the turmeric, salt, coriander, and chili powder in a small bowl and set aside.

*Tempering the ingredients:* In an 8-quart saucepan, heat the oil on high. Once it is hot, add the mustard seeds. When the seeds start to pop, add the hing (if desired), the squash, and the reserved spice mixture. Mix well until the squash is fully coated.

Reduce the heat to medium, cover, and cook for 20 minutes, stirring every 5 minutes to prevent the squash from sticking to the bottom of the pan. After the squash is fully cooked, remove from the heat, sprinkle with the lime juice, and mix well.

Spoon into bowls and garnish with the cilantro.

**Serves 6 to 8.**

# Golden Milk Elixir हल्दी दूध

Turmeric (haldi) has endless health benefits. This miracle spice contains curcumin, a flavonoid that supports a healthy inflammatory response, thereby promoting general well-being. Turmeric also boosts the immune system, assists digestion, purifies the blood, and promotes health of the lungs, circulation system, and nervous system. Turmeric promotes sleep by calming the nervous system, and nutmeg helps with sound sleep, making this recipe the perfect bedtime drink. If you have an upset stomach, this drink will be soothing. Ghee has a laxative effect, so it's great for relieving constipation.

1 cup whole milk (or your choice of milk)

1 teaspoon turmeric powder

¼ teaspoon black pepper

Pinch of cinnamon powder

⅛ teaspoon cardamom powder

2 teaspoons ghee

⅛ teaspoon nutmeg

½ teaspoon of your favorite sweetener (optional)

Place the milk in a saucepan, and cook over medium heat. Add the turmeric, black pepper, cinnamon, cardamom, ghee, nutmeg, and sweetener, and stir. Allow the mixture to simmer for a few minutes, stirring occasionally.

Turn off the heat, and cover. Let it sit for several minutes to allow for greater infusion.

Serve warm and enjoy before bed.

**Serves 1 to 2.**

# Sprouted Mung Salad and Dressing मूंग अंकुरित सलाद

Sprouting is a germinating process and requires planning a couple of days ahead (see more on sprouting on pages 11). This process is therapeutic for me. Watching, nurturing, and facilitating the transformation of seeds into living sprouts is a small and simple pleasure in my life. Sprouting releases the trapped potential of a seed into something beautiful and individually unique. To me, this is an illustration of all life, in that we are budding seeds growing into full expression of our authenticity.

This a beautiful holiday salad, refreshing and healthy. Once sprouted, the mung beans can be stored in a sealed container in the refrigerator for up to a week. There will be leftover sprouted mung beans from this recipe. You can eat them raw, add them to other salads, or make Khitchdi (recipe on page 114) with them.

2 cups whole green mung beans, sprouted*

8 cups water

**Dressing**

½ cup vegetable oil

2 tablespoons hot English mustard

2 tablespoons grated ginger

2 teaspoons ground black or white pepper

1 tablespoon sea salt

3 tablespoons lemon juice

4 green onions with tops, finely chopped

1 serrano chili, diced (optional)

**Salad**

½ cucumber, diced small and water squeezed out

1 red bell pepper, chopped

1 green bell pepper, chopped

½ cup chopped cilantro leaves

Thoroughly wash the mung beans and place in a large bowl with the water. Soak for 8 to 10 hours. The beans will swell and double in size as the water is absorbed. Drain the beans completely in a colander.

Wrap the beans in a moist cheesecloth, tying the cloth tight, and place in a dry bowl. Keep the bowl in a dark, well-ventilated place for 2 days, and allow the beans to germinate. Keep them moist: Every 8 hours, rinse the cheesecloth, drain well, and place in a dry bowl to continue germinating. You will see tiny shoots emerging from the beans.

When they're done sprouting, refrigerate the beans in a sealed plastic bag or container.

*To make the dressing:* Place all the dressing ingredients in a large bowl, and whisk together.

*To make the salad:* Add all the vegetables to the dressing. Add 6 cups of the sprouted mung. Mix thoroughly and enjoy.

**Serves 8 to 10.**

*2 cups of whole mung beans makes 6 cups of sprouted mung beans.

# Fragrant Saffron Basmati Rice केसर चावल

I love the fragrance and taste of saffron and the way it transforms my food. For me, the color of saffron symbolizes the sun, the source of all life and joy on our planet. The spice is the most expensive one in the market and is a great mood enhancer. Recently, I was in Pampore Kashmir, and I saw fields of the light purple crocuses where saffron is harvested from. It was a beautiful sight!

**Tempered ingredients (place each in separate small bowls)**

4 tablespoons ghee

1 teaspoon cumin seeds

2 cinnamon sticks

2 cardamom pods, green or brown

2 bay leaves

3 cups uncooked basmati rice

1 cup peas

6 cups water

1 tablespoon salt

½ teaspoon saffron

*Tempering the ingredients:* Heat the ghee in an 8-quart saucepan on high. When the ghee is hot, add the cumin seeds. While they are popping, add the cinnamon sticks, cardamoms, and bay leaves.

Immediately add the rice and peas, and stir-fry for 30 seconds, until coated with the ghee and spice mixture.

Add the water and salt and bring to a boil. Once boiling, reduce the heat to medium. Add the saffron and simmer for 15 minutes, until almost all the water is absorbed. Do not stir.

Turn off the heat, cover, and steam for 10 minutes longer, undisturbed. Do not lift the cover while steaming. Serve hot.

**Serves 6 to 8.**

*You can use leftovers later or cut the recipe in half if the serving size is too large.*

# Massoor Dahl with Spinach मसूर दाल

Dahl, which is lentils of any kind, is considered an essential component of an Indian menu. Massoor dahl is a staple across India because of its ability to cook quickly on the stove within 20 to 25 minutes, without a pressure cooker. It is known in the United States as brown lentils, available in grocery stores. In India, these lentils are split and husked to reveal a pink-salmon color. They are easy to cook, easy to digest, and delicious. This dish is common in many arid villages where nature has not been kind. (See Dahl Chart on page 12.)

1 ½ cups red lentils

8–10 cups water (divided)

**Spice mixture**

1 tablespoon red chili powder

3 tablespoons ground coriander

2 teaspoons roasted cumin powder (or try Bina's Roasted Cumin)

1 tablespoon salt (or to taste)

1 bay leaf

3 tablespoons ghee

1 medium onion, diced

1 ½ cups chopped fresh (or frozen) baby spinach

1 tablespoon tomato paste

1 tablespoon lemon juice

½ cup chopped mint leaves

Soak the lentils overnight in 2 cups of the water.

*To make the spice mixture:* Measure the red chili powder, coriander, cumin, and salt into a bowl and set aside.

In an 8-quart saucepan, bring the lentils, bay leaf, and 4 cups of the water to a boil on high. Reduce the heat to medium, cover, and allow to simmer, stirring every 20 minutes and adding the remaining 2-4 cups water if needed. Once cooked, remove from the heat. Take a potato masher or the side of a large ladle and partially mash the beans to make a thick consistency. Set aside in the saucepan.

Heat the ghee in a small skillet on medium-high. Sauté the onions for 12 to 15 minutes, until translucent. Add the onions to the lentil mixture. Stir in the reserved spice mixture and mix well.

Return the lentil mixture to medium-high, then add the spinach, tomato paste, and lemon juice and mix well. Continue to stir and cook until it simmers.

Garnish with the mint. Serve with saffron rice.

**Serves 8.**

# Macchi (Fish) मछली

India is a subcontinent surrounded by water—the Arabian Sea to the west and the Bay of Bengal to the east—and blessed with many rivers. It is no wonder that fish and seafood are a staple of all coastal towns and areas. I am very proud of this recipe. Whenever I make it, I receive amazing compliments.

1 tablespoon salt (or to taste)

½ teaspoon red chili powder

½ teaspoon ground black pepper

1 tablespoon tandoori masala powder

1 ⅓ pounds cod or other white fish

6 tablespoons ghee

½ cup small-diced onions

¼ cup small-diced celery

¼ cup small-diced bell peppers

4 tablespoons rice flour

4 cups fish stock (1 teaspoon HonDashi soup stock plus 2 cups hot water)

½ chopped green onions

In a small bowl, combine the salt, chili powder, black pepper, and tandoori powder. Sprinkle on both sides of the fish.

Heat the ghee on high in a flat, deep 16-inch skillet with a lid. Once it is hot, add the onions, celery, and peppers. Sauté for 10 to 12 minutes, stirring occasionally, until the onion is translucent. Add the rice flour and stir to coat the vegetables. Add the fish stock and simmer for 5 minutes, stirring constantly. Reduce the heat to medium-low.

Cut the fish into even pieces (6 inches wide), and place them in the sauce. Cover and cook, without turning, for 6 to 8 minutes; this requires judgment depending on how thick the fish is. Do not overcook the fish.

Garnish with the green onions. Serve with Mango Pomegranate Salad (recipe on page 144).

**Serves 4.**

# Mango Pomegranate Salad आम अनार सलाद

I love this salad. It is refreshingly vibrant and colorful, and a great accompaniment to Macchi (recipe on page 141). A breeze to make, this pairs well with any side dish, or enjoy it on its own. I recommend substituting dried cranberries if pomegranates are not in season.

1 tablespoon lemon juice

1 tablespoon rice wine vinegar

1 teaspoon salt

¼ teaspoon ground black pepper

1 ripe mango, peeled and diced

½ cup pomegranate seeds

½ cup diced red bell peppers

12 small cherry tomatoes, cut in half

½ cup small-diced red onions

1 serrano chili, diced small

½ cup chopped mint leaves

In a large bowl, mix the lemon juice, vinegar, salt, and black pepper. Add the remaining ingredients and mix well. Let marinate in the refrigerator for 1 to 2 hours before serving.

**Serves 4.**

# Coconut Burfi (Kopra Pak) नारियल बरफी

This is a sweet, golden, saffron-infused treat that's the perfect end to a delicious meal. Coconut is a healthy fat that supports the immune system, improves digestion and absorption of nutrients, and provides a natural source of quick energy and vitality. For convenience, fresh unsweetened coconut is available in the frozen section of Indian food stores.

3 cups water

1 ½ cups sugar (or to taste)

½ teaspoon saffron

1 teaspoon lemon juice

2 teaspoons ghee

4 cups shredded unsweetened coconut

½ cup golden raisins

1 ½ cups ricotta cheese

1 cup dry milk powder

1 tablespoon cardamom powder (reserve ¼ teaspoon for garnish)

3 tablespoons crushed pistachios and almonds (reserve 1 tablespoon for garnish)

In a 4-quart saucepan, heat the water and sugar on high until the syrup boils and bubbles appear. Reduce the heat to medium, and simmer until the water reduces to 1 ½ cups. Add the saffron and lemon juice and cook for 3 minutes.

Heat the ghee in a 12-inch skillet on medium. Add the coconut and raisins, coating the coconut with ghee, and cook for 1 minute. Add the sugar syrup and cook for 1 minute, stirring constantly until well blended. Mix in the ricotta and milk powder and simmer for 3 to 5 minutes. Add the cardamom and nuts (less the amounts reserved for garnishing).

Spread the mixture in a pie dish and decorate with the reserved cardamom and crushed nuts. Refrigerate until the mixture sets, then cut into squares to serve as a dessert.

**Serves 8.**

Many Americans have adopted an eat-on-the-run breakfast lifestyle—grab a piece of toast or bagel and a cup of coffee, and eat mindlessly in the car while on the phone and rushing to work. On the other hand, Indians take their breakfast—like they take all food—very seriously. In India, the first meal of the day is a piping-hot dish served with seasonal fruit, chai, sprouted mung, and chutneys. It is a time when the family dines together before beginning their day. A warm meal first thing kindles your digestion if you take the time to eat it with reverence.

A breakfast buffet at a hotel in India is quite the culinary feast—a mind-boggling array of choices that reflect the culture and diversity of every state and region. I am always amazed and perplexed by the crazy number of options—I want to try them all, but of course that is impossible!

In this section, I have offered some popular recipes and childhood favorites for you to enjoy. Sprinkled throughout the other menus in this book are many breakfast options as well. To name a few: dosas and coconut chutneys, idlis and sambhar, mung dahl dosa and green chutney, sprouted mung and chana salad, parathas and yogurt raitas, and puris with potatoes and peas. All provide a healthy start to your day.

# Chapter 8

# Indian Breakfasts

Parathas Stuffed with Radishes    150
Potato Pattice                    152
Akuri Scrambled Eggs              153
Black Chana Salad                 155
Vitamin Bhel Salad                158
Upma                              159
Chole                             161

# Parathas Stuffed with Radishes मूली पराठा

Parathas are a North Indian specialty and a popular breakfast staple. They are made from unleavened dough, which can be stuffed with a variety of fillings such as cauliflower, radishes, and spices. They are then shallow-fried in a pan and spread with melted ghee before serving. Want to eat the best parathas on the planet? Chandni Chowk in Old Delhi has a quaint little alley called Paratha Gali, where the locals line up early in the morning to choose from at least 50 different fillings.

### Filling

2 cups grated white daikon (large white radish)

½ teaspoon salt

2 tablespoons finely chopped cilantro leaves

1 tablespoon garam masala (or try Bina's Bombay or Garam Masala)

### Dough

3 cups whole wheat flour

⅛ cup ghee

⅛ cup sunflower oil

1 tablespoon salt

1 ½ cups water

½ cup wheat flour (for rolling)

8 tablespoons ghee

*To make the filling:* Place the daikon in a medium bowl and sprinkle with the salt. Allow to stand for 3 minutes.

Take handfuls of the daikon and squeeze out all the excess water. (See box on page 151.) Once the liquid is drained from the daikon, add the cilantro and garam masala and mix well. Set aside.

*To make the dough:* Mix together the flour, ghee, oil, and salt in a large bowl. Carefully add the water in ½ cup increments, and knead the dough to blend all the ingredients to avoid lumps. Continue kneading to make a smooth dough. Allow the dough to sit for 30 minutes, covered.

Divide the dough into 12 portions. On a floured surface, use a rolling pin to roll each portion into 5-to-6-inch-round circles.

Place 1 ½ tablespoons of the daikon mixture in the middle of one circle. Cover the mixture by drawing the edges toward the center. Preheat a flat griddle on medium-high.

*continued on page 151*

*continued from page 150*

While the griddle is preheating, roll the filled dough in flour, place back on the floured surface, and roll out again gently into a 4-to-5-inch-round circle. Roll lightly so that the filling doesn't squeeze out.

Place the paratha on the preheated griddle.

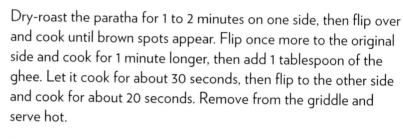

Dry-roast the paratha for 1 to 2 minutes on one side, then flip over and cook until brown spots appear. Flip once more to the original side and cook for 1 minute longer, then add 1 tablespoon of the ghee. Let it cook for about 30 seconds, then flip to the other side and cook for about 20 seconds. Remove from the griddle and serve hot.

Repeat this process for each dough portion. If the griddle is big enough, you can cook several at a time.

Serve hot with dahl or Potato Raita with Hot Mustard (recipe on page 107).

**Serves 6 to 8.**

*When you add salt to grated daikon, it starts to release its excess water. It is crucial to remove this excess water from the filling before rolling out the paratha dough. The water will make the dough wet and difficult to roll.*

*Also, you can substitute grated cauliflower for the daikon.*

# Potato Pattice आलू टिक्का

This is an Indian version of American hash browns. These potato patties, considered street food, are sold at food carts in northern India. They're known as ragda pattice or aloo tiki on Chowpatty Beach in Mumbai. They can be served with meat, eggs, chole, and a variety of chutneys—pecan, amchur, and cilantro—and can be garnished with cheese, raw onions, cilantro, and a slice of lime. Fresh Mint and Green Onion Raita (recipe on page 167) is another delicious accompaniment. Potato Pattice is also great as an appetizer!

3 pounds potatoes (about 6 medium)

½ cup arrowroot

1 tablespoon salt

1 tablespoon lime juice

½ cup sunflower oil (divided)

In a large pot, boil the potatoes with skins on, covered, for 20 to 25 minutes.* Rinse with cold water until you can hold the potatoes. Peel and mash the potatoes using a potato ricer, cheese grater, or potato masher.

While the potatoes are warm, add the arrowroot, salt, and lime juice. Form into 3-inch smooth patties like mini burgers. At this point, the patties can be stored in the fridge until needed.

Heat an electric Teflon-coated 12-inch skillet on high. Add 3 tablespoons of the oil to the skillet. When hot, put 3 to 4 potato patties on the skillet and cook the first side for 12 minutes, or until brown. Add another tablespoon of oil for crispness. Flip to the other side and cook for another 12 minutes, or until brown. Serve hot.

**Makes 14 to 16 patties.**

*You can use a pressure cooker to speed the cooking of the potatoes. Place whole washed, unpeeled potatoes in the pressure cooker with water (follow the cooker's directions). When they're done, drain the potatoes, then peel and mash them to the consistency of mashed potatoes.

# Akuri Scrambled Eggs with Cilantro and Ginger  आकुरी

Akuri are scrambled eggs infused with fragrant herbs and spices. When I make them for my children and guests, they cannot stop eating them! We adopted this recipe from the Iranians (or Parsi) who were granted asylum on the northwestern shore of India after being ousted from their homeland by the Turks. We call this recipe "green eggs."

8 whole eggs + 2 egg yolks

¼ cup milk

½ teaspoon salt

½ teaspoon ground black pepper

3 tablespoons ghee or butter

1 tablespoon minced ginger

4 tablespoons minced green onions, with tops

½ teaspoon turmeric powder

1–2 tablespoons minced serrano chilies (optional)

4 tablespoons finely chopped cilantro leaves

½ teaspoon roasted cumin powder (try Bina's Roasted Cumin)

½ tomato, thinly sliced

In a small bowl, whisk the eggs, milk, salt, and pepper. It should be well combined, but do not overbeat.

In a heavy 10-inch skillet, heat the ghee or butter on medium-high, until it melts. Add the ginger and fry for 10 seconds. Add the green onions and fry for 1 minute, until soft but not brown. Stirring constantly, add the turmeric, serrano chilies (if desired), and cilantro and cook for 30 seconds.

Reduce the heat to medium-low. Immediately pour in the egg mixture. Stir the mixture constantly with a whisk, making sure to scrape the sides continuously, in a figure-eight motion, until the eggs begin to form moist, soft, creamy curds. Remove from the heat to avoid overcooking once the curds appear.

Immediately place eggs in a serving dish. Garnish with the cumin and tomatoes.

**Serves 4 to 6.**

*Blasting the eggs on high heat and cooking in a hurry will cause your curds to become rubbery. Keep the heat low to get loose, small curds—it will look like a lumpy custard.*

# Black Chana Salad  काला चना सलाद

Want to lose weight? Looking for an easy, tasty, and healthy recipe? Here it is, a low-fat salad packed with vitamins, minerals, fiber, and protein! It's a great breakfast alternative that will leave you feeling fresh and clean. It's also wonderful food for a cleanse. Sprouting the chickpeas provides immense health benefits (read more about sprouting on page 11). This salad usually tastes better the next day as it marinates.

2 cups black chickpeas (chana)

8 cups water

1 tablespoon salt

1 bunch scallions, with tops, finely chopped

1 bunch cilantro leaves, finely chopped

2 serrano chilies, diced small (optional)

1 lemon or lime, squeezed

In a large bowl, soak the chickpeas in the water overnight.

The next day, place the beans and water in a large pot and add the salt. Cook on medium-high, covered, for 55 minutes, until soft. Drain the beans in a colander, then place in a large serving bowl.

Add the scallions, cilantro, and serrano chilies (if desired) and mix well. Add the lemon juice and more salt, if needed, adjusting to your taste.

**Serves 6 to 8.**

# Vitamin Bhel Salad  विटामिन भेल सलाद

**This recipe needs a little bit of planning because the sprouting requires 1 to 2 days. This is a living power food.**

## Sprouting

2 cups black chickpeas (chana)

9 cups water (divided; for sprouting the beans)

1 cup whole mung beans

16 cups water (for cooking the sprouted beans)

1 tablespoon salt

## Dressing

½ cup vegetable oil

1 ½ tablespoons mustard powder

2 tablespoons grated ginger

1 bunch green onions, with tops, finely chopped

1 red onion, finely chopped

1 cup chopped, packed cilantro leaves

1 cup chopped, packed mint leaves

1 tablespoon chaat masala (or try Bina's Bombay Masala)

1 ½ tablespoons salt

1 tablespoon ground black pepper

*To sprout:* Place the black chickpeas in an extra-large bowl with 5 cups of the water. In a separate extra-large bowl, place the mung beans in the remaining 4 cups water. Soak both for at least 8 hours or overnight. (Note: The beans will absorb the water and expand. Do not soak longer than an overnight period because this can cause the beans to rot and ferment.)

Drain each separately and place them in separate moist cheesecloths or breathable cotton cloths and tie at the ends. Place in separate bowls in a dark place. Every 6 hours, moisten the chickpeas and beans in the cloth and thoroughly drain all the water before returning them to the dark place.

Keep them in the dark place for 1 to 2 days, until they germinate and start to sprout. Once they have sprouted, place them in the refrigerator. (Note: Use the sprouted beans and chickpeas within 7 days.)

In an 8-quart saucepan, bring the 16 cups water and the salt to a boil. Add the sprouted chickpeas and boil for 5 to 8 minutes. Add the sprouted mung beans to the pan with the chickpeas and boil for another 5 minutes. Remove from the heat, rinse with cold water, and drain. Set aside.

*To make the dressing:* Mix all the dressing ingredients in a large bowl.

Add the chickpeas and mung beans, mix well, and let marinate in the refrigerator for up to 8 hours. Serve cold.

**Serves 8 to 10.**

# Upma (Indian Cream of Wheat or farina) उपमा

Cream of Wheat in India is known as sooji and is available in Indian grocery stores. I grew up with this breakfast dish in my home, and I love it. It's comforting and filling as a savory dish with vegetables and spices. It's wonderful with plain yogurt. The combination of Cream of Wheat and yogurt is high in protein, fiber, vitamin D, calcium, and iron. For gluten-free options, make it with Cream of Rice or quinoa. It works!

2 cups instant Cream of Wheat or Cream of Rice

**Tempering ingredients (place each in separate small bowls)**

⅓ cup ghee

½ teaspoon cumin seeds

¾ teaspoon mustard seeds

10 curry leaves

1 tablespoon grated ginger

1 small serrano chili, diced

1 medium onion, diced small

10–12 cashews

½ cup grated carrots

1 cup peas

5 cups water (or 2 cups plain yogurt plus 3 cups water)

1 ½ tablespoons salt (or to taste)

½ cup chopped cilantro leaves

1 lime, cut in wedges

In a medium pot on medium heat, add the Cream of Wheat and toast for 3 minutes, stirring constantly, until it looks dry and separate. Do not burn. Remove from the heat and transfer to a plate. Set aside.

*Tempering the ingredients:* In the same pot, heat the ghee to medium-high but not smoking. Add the cumin and mustard seeds and heat until they pop. Immediately add the curry leaves, ginger, and serrano chilies, and sauté for 30 seconds.

Add the onions and cashews and sauté for 8 to 10 minutes until the onions turn translucent. Then add the carrots and peas and cook for 3 minutes, mixing everything together.

Add the Cream of Wheat and the water (or yogurt-water). Stir constantly on medium-high to avoid lumps. Add the salt.

Reduce the heat and simmer for 4 minutes, stirring constantly so the mixture does not stick to the pan. The Cream of Wheat will absorb moisture, swell, and start to cook. Turn off the burner, cover, and let rest for 8 to 10 minutes, to allow steam to finish the cooking, until all the water is absorbed.

Serve hot. Garnish with the cilantro, and squeeze lime wedges over top. Serve with plain Yogurt (recipe on page 115).

**Serves 6.**

# Chole (Garbanzo Beans) छोले

This is an irresistible street food with a sweet, sour, and pungent taste. Chole can be a great breakfast accompanied with rice and naan or parathas. Pour chole over the Potato Pattice (recipe on page 152) and garnish with generous dollops of Green Cilantro Chutney (recipe on page 200) and Amchur Chutney (recipe on page 199).

2 cups uncooked garbanzo beans

10 cups water (divided)

1 teaspoon turmeric powder

1 tablespoon salt

1 tablespoon grated ginger

1 black tea bag, sealed in a tea infuser

1 tablespoon ground coriander

1 teaspoon roasted cumin powder (try Bina's Roasted Cumin)

2 teaspoons amchur powder

1 tablespoon garam masala (try Bina's Garam Masala)

**Tempering ingredients (place each in separate small bowls)**

2 tablespoons ghee

½ teaspoon cumin seeds

Pinch of hing

1 bay leaf

2 tablespoons lemon juice

½ bunch cilantro leaves, finely chopped

2 cups finely diced onions

2 limes, cut in 6 segments

2 serrano chilies, finely diced (optional)

Soak the garbanzo beans in 4 cups of the water for at least 8 to 10 hours or overnight.

Put the soaked beans in a pressure cooker with the remaining 6 cups water, the turmeric, salt, ginger, and tea bag in sealed tea infuser for 20 minutes, until it whistles. Without forcing it, allow the pressure cooker to open. Let the pressure dissipate for 10 minutes in the cooker. Discard the tea infuser.

The beans should be fully cooked. Take a potato masher and partially mash the garbanzos for a thicker consistency. Mix in the coriander, cumin, amchur, and garam masala.

*Tempering the ingredients:* In a large pan, heat the ghee over high heat. When it's hot, add the cumin seeds. When they start to splutter, quickly add the hing and bay leaf.

Add to the garbanzo beans along with the lemon juice and mix.

Serve garnished with the cilantro, onions, limes, and serrano chilies (if desired).

**Serves 8 to 10.**

The word *party* took on a profound meaning for me after I was convinced to take a Disney cruise with my friends Rick and Karen. At first, I resisted—I told my husband we should go someplace else. But my friends, who are avid Disney fans, taught us to loosen up and that we deserve to have laughter and fun in our lives. It was an experience being on that cruise, where the atmosphere of fun, dance, music, laughter, and joy was electric and contagious. I was pleasantly surprised to discover that we are all kids at heart, and, due to the trials and tribulations of our life journey, we have forgotten how to play as adults. It is time to bring back that simple, innocent, uninhibited fun that kids naturally have. We are privy to that too as adults!

A party to me now and always is to draw and encourage conversations with friends, family, and acquaintances in my kitchen. By eating and drinking, enjoying music and laughter, we honor loving and meaningful relationships and create magical, precious, and memorable moments together. I have always loved cooking, and my husband and I would rather share meals with friends than eat alone. We recently formed a gourmet club with three other couples. We meet once every two months and share wonderful meals based on a theme that was chosen. Occasions such as these are unforgettable, and long-lasting friendships are made under these circumstances.

In India, celebrations, rituals, parties, and special moments are always centered around food. Food is a way of life and love and hospitality. As soon as a guest arrives, food and chai are offered. You'd better learn to say "enough" in India, or else your plate will get refilled all the time and you'll soon be bursting at the seams.

In this chapter, I offer to you a simple party menu to enjoy with your loved ones and friends—and maybe even to help you recapture moments of joy and laughter and make some memories.

# Chapter 9

# Party Menu

Baby Rack of Lamb                       166
Fresh Mint and Green Onion Raita        167
Chapatti                                168
Bina's Okra                             170
Eggplant Rice                           171
Mung Dahl Bhajias                       174
Rajma Dahl                              175

# Baby Rack of Lamb मेमने का रैक

This is a complex, fragrant, flavorful lamb appetizer and yet simple to make. Eat them like lollipops by dipping them in the sauce and spices. They are a hit at parties because of the lingering flavors of salty, sour, and earthy that sing on the palate. Do not overcook lamb; it likes to be cooked medium-rare for perfection, and if overcooked, it loses its juiciness and is a bit chewy. I made this recipe for our gourmet club by varying some ingredients in the marinade to make it more Mediterranean, since that was our theme that month. It was still outstanding—everyone raved about it.

8 tablespoons olive oil

2 tablespoons lemon juice

¼ cup water

10 cloves garlic, minced

½ cup mint leaves

1 tablespoon salt

2 teaspoons ground black pepper

3 teaspoons ground coriander

2 teaspoons roasted cumin powder (or try Bina's Roasted Cumin)

2 tablespoons paprika

1 teaspoon red chili powder

4 pounds baby rack of lamb

Lamb Dipping Sauce (see page 167)

Additional Dipping Spices (see page 167)

To the bowl of a food processor, add the oil, lemon juice, water, garlic, mint, salt, black pepper, coriander, cumin, paprika, and red chili powder. Blend into a smooth paste.

Rinse the lamb, and pat dry. Lightly score the fat on the lamb to ensure that the spices penetrate, but do not remove the fat. Spread the marinade all over the lamb and massage it into the lamb. Place in a large resealable plastic bag and refrigerate for 6 to 8 hours.

When you're ready to grill, bring the lamb to room temperature. Remove from the marinade, and save the leftover marinade for basting. Wrap foil around each bone tip to prevent burning.

Preheat the grill on the highest temperature. When ready, place the lamb with the outer, fattier side down on the grill, cover, and cook for 6 minutes. Baste once, midway, with the leftover marinade. Flip the lamb racks, cover, and cook for another 6 minutes. (If the lamb burns, turn the heat down to medium and move to a cooler side of the grill.) Baste again midway with the leftover marinade. Lamb should be cooked to medium-rare.

When the lamb is done cooking, transfer it to a cutting board, and allow it to sit for 10 minutes. Cut into individual chops, and serve with the Lamb Dipping Sauce and Additional Dipping Spices.

**Serves 6 to 8.**

*continued on page 167*

continued from page 166

## Lamb Dipping Sauce

1 onion, finely chopped

2 cloves garlic

½ cup lime juice

16 mint leaves

4 cups vegetable broth

3 tablespoons ghee

Place the onion, garlic, lime juice, mint, and broth in a blender and blend until smooth.

In a 4-quart saucepan, heat the ghee on medium-high until hot. Add the blended ingredients, and bring to a boil. Reduce the heat to medium, and simmer for 5 minutes, allowing some of the liquid to evaporate.

## Additional Dipping Spices

3 tablespoons roasted cumin powder (or try Bina's Roasted Cumin)

3 tablespoons crystallized salt

Place the cumin and salt in separate small serving bowls. Dip the lamb chops into the dipping sauce, then lightly press it into the cumin bowl and then the salt bowl—and enjoy the lamb lollipops!

## Fresh Mint and Green Onion Raita मिंट रायता

There are many raitas to choose from in this book. This one is quick and easy to make and pairs especially well with the "lollipop" lamb chops (see page 166). The mint in the yogurt is very refreshing with the lamb. Chaat masala is easily found in Indian grocery stores.

4 cups plain yogurt

1 cup chopped mint leaves

½ cup finely minced green onions with tops

½ tablespoon salt

½ teaspoon chaat masala (or try Bina's Bombay Masala)

Place the yogurt in a large bowl and whisk until lumps disappear. Add the mint, green onions, salt, and chaat masala, and mix well with a spoon.

Refrigerate until ready to serve.

**Serves 6 to 8.**

# Chapatti (Unleavened Bread) रोटी

Roti, rotli, phulka, or chapatti—this round, flat unleavened bread known by different names is a staple of India. It's made with wheat flour and roasted on a griddle, then topped with ghee. It is served with vegetables, meat, and dahl, and can be used as a wrap. You can also break off a piece of the chapatti and scoop the vegetables and meat, or dip it in dahl or raita. This is a traditional method of eating with the fingers. It takes some getting used to, but I think it makes the food taste better.

2 cups whole wheat flour, plus extra for dusting

½ teaspoon salt

2 tablespoons ghee or vegetable oil

1 cup water

Place the flour in a large bowl, and make a well in the center of the flour. Add the salt and ghee or oil to the well and mix thoroughly. Add ½ cup of the water and knead into a dough. The water will start to bind the flour. Then add the remaining ½ cup water and continue to knead until smooth. You should have a soft, pliable dough to work with. Let the dough sit, covered, for about 20 minutes.

Roll the dough into balls 3 inches in diameter. Turn two stove burners on medium-high at the same time. Place a 10-inch skillet on one burner and a metal cooling rack on the other.

Coat the balls of dough with flour to prevent sticking while rolling. On a lightly floured surface, use a rolling pin to roll the dough into flat circles. Each chapatti should be about 6 inches in diameter and ⅛ inch thick.

Place one chapatti on the hot skillet. As soon as you see bubbles start to form, flip the chapatti over. The second side should only cook for 30 to 45 seconds. Use tongs to pick up the chapatti without puncturing it, and place the first-cooked side down on the heated metal rack. Now you will see the bread start to puff up, and air will steam out of the side. Use the tongs to turn it on the other side for just a few seconds. Remove the chapatti from the heat with the tongs and place on a plate.

Spread with ghee while hot, and serve hot with any vegetable or dahl.

**Makes 12.**

# Bina's Okra भिंडी

Small, tender okra is grown year-round all over India. It is a favorite of all the kids. The versatility and texture of this great side dish works well with rice, lentils, or the protein of your choice. It tastes great with naans, puris, and parathas, and any of your favorite raitas from this book.

8 cups fresh okra

4 cups vegetable oil

1 tablespoon masala (or try Bina's Bombay Masala or Bina's Maharani Masala)*

Wash and trim the okra, and cut into thirds. Place on paper towels to dry completely.

Heat the oil in a Dutch oven or a wok (kadhai) on medium-high until the temperature is 350–375 degrees (see How to Deep-Fry on page 17). Oil must be hot but not smoking before frying, and must maintain the same temperature. To test the oil for readiness, drop a small piece of the okra in the oil. If the okra starts to sizzle and floats to the top, it is ready.

When the oil is ready, add half of the okra and cook on high for 15 minutes, stirring every 3 minutes, until crispy. Remove from the oil using a slotted spoon or spider skimmer. Allow the excess oil to drain into the pan. Place the okra on a paper towel to soak up the oil.

Sprinkle the masala on the okra while warm.

Cook the second half of the okra the same way.

**Serves 4 to 6.**

*If you don't have masala or Bina's spice blend on hand, combine 1 teaspoon salt, 2 teaspoons amchur powder, 2 teaspoons red chili powder, and 2 teaspoons ground fennel.

# Eggplant Rice बैंगन चावल

This my version of a one-pot ratatouille. I like to make this dish for vegetarians. The fragrance is so appetizing! Serve it with Fresh Mint and Green Onion Raita (recipe on page 167) for a complete light meal.

**Tempering ingredients (place each in separate small bowls)**

½ cup vegetable oil or coconut oil

½ teaspoon mustard seeds

½ teaspoon cumin seeds

10–12 curry leaves

1 serrano chili, sliced in half

2 cinnamon sticks

Pinch of hing (optional)

1 medium eggplant, cut into 1-inch pieces with skin (about 6 cups)

1 red bell pepper, diced

1 green bell pepper, diced

1 cup peas

3 cups uncooked basmati rice

1 teaspoon turmeric powder

2 teaspoons fennel seeds

1 tablespoon garam masala (or try Bina's Garam Masala)

1 teaspoon red pepper flakes

¾ tablespoon salt (or to taste)

5 ½ cups water

*Tempering the ingredients:* In an 8-quart saucepan, heat the oil on medium-high until hot. Add the mustard seeds, cumin seeds, curry leaves, serrano chili, cinnamon, and hing (if desired).

When the seeds start to pop, immediately add the eggplant and cook for 11 minutes, until it breaks down. Add the bell peppers and peas and stir. Let it cook for 2 minutes.

Add the rice and stir to coat all the ingredients. Stir in the turmeric, fennel seeds, garam masala, red pepper flakes, and salt.

Add the water, increase the heat to high, and bring to a boil. When it's boiling, reduce the heat to medium and simmer, uncovered, for 10 to 15 minutes. Then cover the pot, remove from the heat, and allow the rice to finish cooking undisturbed for 20 minutes. Do not stir or lift the lid while it's steaming.

**Serves 8.**

# Mung Dahl Bhajias मुंग भजिया

These fried dumplings are made like falafel and look like mini falafel. One of the best things about this recipe is it's a great appetizer and goes well with any of my chutneys, especially amchur, cilantro, tamarind, and date. They are so delicious you can't stop eating them. This can be made 3 days ahead of time. Just put the batter in the fridge, and when you're ready, bring the batter to room temperature and deep-fry this addictively crunchy snack.

2 cups split mung dahl with green husks

6 cups water

**Dry-roasted spices**

8 tablespoons coriander seeds

2 tablespoons cumin seeds

5 dried red chilies

10 black peppercorns

1 ½ tablespoons salt

1 ½ tablespoons sunflower oil

1 teaspoon baking soda

¼ cup rice flour

3 cups vegetable oil

Place the split mung dahl with husks in a large bowl or pot with the water and soak for 8 to 10 hours or overnight.

Drain, reserving 1 cup of the water for blending, and place the mung dahl in a blender or food processor. Blend coarsely to make a thick paste. If it's too thick to blend well, add water in ¼ cup increments. Use as little water as possible. Return it to the large bowl, cover, and put in a warm, dark place to allow it to ferment for at least 6 to 8 hours.

*To dry-roast the spices:* In a small saucepan on medium-high, dry-roast the coriander seeds, cumin seeds, chilies, and peppercorns for 6 to 8 minutes, or until the fragrance is released. Remove from the heat and let cool. Grind the cooled spices in a coffee grinder to a smooth powder.

Mix the spices into the mung dahl after it has finished fermenting. Add the salt, sunflower oil, baking soda, and rice flour, and mix well. The batter is now ready. You can save it in the refrigerator for 3 days or prepare the bhajias immediately.

Heat the vegetable oil in a wok or Dutch oven (kadhai) on medium-high. Make sure the oil temperature is between 350 and 400 degrees. To test whether it is hot enough for frying, add by a drop of the batter to the pan. If it is hot enough, the batter will start to bubble and rise to the surface. If it is not ready, it will sink to the bottom (see How to Deep-Fry on page 17).

Once the oil is hot, drop 2 tablespoons of the batter at a time into the oil, making sure the dumplings are not touching each other. Cook for 2 to 4 minutes, or until crispy and golden brown on the outside. Remove with a slotted spoon or a spider skimmer, and place on a paper towel to drain and cool.

**Serves 6 to 8.**

# Rajma Dahl राजमा

This is an Indian version of red beans and rice, which is a staple of the people living in Punjab. It is eaten with naans or parathas. This "poor man's food" is served in dhabas, or food stalls, along highways and interstates. Travelers look forward to stopping at their favorite dhaba to eat this finger-licking delicacy. If you are in a hurry, after the soaking process, you can use a pressure cooker instead of a slow cooker and then follow the rest of the recipe steps for beans to complete it. Dried kidney beans, known as rajma beans, can be found in ethnic Indian grocery stores.

2 cups rajma (dried kidney beans)

¼ cup whole urad dahl (or black dahl; see Dahl Chart on page 12)

8 cups water

1 tablespoon salt

1 tablespoon grated ginger

1 bay leaf

3 tablespoons tomato paste

**Tempering ingredients (place each in separate small bowls)**

2 tablespoons ghee or oil

½ teaspoon cumin seeds

1 tablespoon garam masala (or try Bina's Garam Masala)

1 teaspoon red chili powder

Cilantro leaves

Place the rajma and urad dahl in a large pot with the water. Soak for 8 to 10 hours or overnight. (The beans will double in size.) Do not drain the water.

Turn the slow cooker on high. Put the beans and the soaking water, salt, ginger, and bay leaf in the slow cooker and cook for 2 hours. Reduce the temperature to low and cook for another 6 hours. Do not stir or open during the entire cooking process.

Open the slow cooker, and while the beans are warm, take a potato masher or the side of a ladle and partially mash the beans to make a thick consistency. Add the tomato paste and mix well.

*Tempering the ingredients:* In a small saucepan, heat the ghee or oil on medium-high until hot but not smoking. Add the cumin seeds and cook until they start to pop. Remove from the heat and stir the cumin into the bean mixture.

Add the garam masala and chili powder, and mix well. Turn the slow cooker to low for 1 hour.

Serve garnished with cilantro.

**Serves 6 to 8.**

India is a land of fairs, festivals, rituals, and celebrations—frequent, boisterous events with songs, dances, feasts, and prayers at their essence. In this land of contrasts and contradictions, everything is considered sacred. People have a reverence and zest for life, and they're always celebrating something: birthdays, Diwali, festival of lights, Holi, festival of colors, Christmas, New Year, harvest festival, the full moon, the new moon—the list goes on. If Indians had their way, every day would be a holiday.

In this spirit, I have added an Indian flair to the celebration of America's independence, the 4th of July. I have resided many more years in the United States than I lived in India, and so it is now my adopted country. I was inspired to add some of India's energy, color, and texture into this menu.

We have celebrated the 4th in our home for years by inviting friends and family for feasting, fun, and laughter. After dessert, it's off to the park to see the fireworks. I have taken traditional barbecue fare—corn, chicken, lamb, beef, watermelon, potatoes, cabbage—and added my ethnic twist by enhancing the flavors with spices, aromatics, and herbs. The result is a creative menu of favorite meats and vegetables that are colorful and vibrant. It's just another way to live joyfully! Besides the menu in this chapter, you can pick and choose favorite recipes from other chapters to add to your holiday spread.

Chapter 10

# 4<sup>th</sup> of July Indian Style

| | |
|---|---|
| Indian Fajitas | 180 |
| Grilled Spiced Corn | 181 |
| Mung Dahl with Chana Dahl | 184 |
| Cucumber Raita | 185 |
| East Indian Coleslaw | 188 |
| Bina's Yellow Potatoes | 189 |
| Seekh Kebabs | 192 |
| Watermelon Juice | 193 |

# Indian Fajitas देसी फाहिता

A twist on a Mexican favorite, Indian Fajitas are a great option for those who don't want to grill. Super convenient, this dish can be stir-fried quickly on party day. But plan a couple of days ahead for marinating the meat and vegetables.

3 ¼ pounds boneless, skinless chicken thighs and breasts, sliced*

1 red onion, sliced

½ red bell pepper, sliced

½ orange bell pepper, sliced

½ green bell pepper, sliced

2 tablespoons chopped garlic

2 tablespoons grated ginger

¼ cup chopped cilantro leaves

¼ cup chopped mint leaves

2 tablespoons lemon juice (or to taste)

3 tablespoons mustard oil

1 tablespoon salt (or to taste)

2 tablespoons tandoori masala powder

1 tablespoon roasted cumin powder (or try Bina's Roasted Cumin)

2 tablespoons ground coriander

2 tablespoons garam masala (or try Bina's Garam Masala)

½ cup vegetable oil or coconut oil (or another oil with a high frying temperature)

Add all the ingredients except the oil to a gallon-size resealable plastic bag. Massage the ingredients in the bag to ensure absorption. Let marinate in the refrigerator for 4 to 8 hours, occasionally massaging the ingredients.

At least 1 hour before cooking, remove the bag from the refrigerator to bring the ingredients to room temperature. Drain the liquid.

Heat a deep 12-inch skillet on high and add the oil. When the oil is hot, carefully add all the marinated ingredients, and stir-fry for 10 minutes, or until fully cooked.

Serve with chapattis or corn tortillas.

**Serves 6 to 8.**

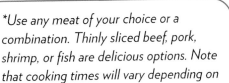

*Use any meat of your choice or a combination. Thinly sliced beef, pork, shrimp, or fish are delicious options. Note that cooking times will vary depending on the meat you use.

# Grilled Spiced Corn भुना मसालेदार मकाई

A variation on grilled corn on the cob, this is a street food in India. July is the perfect time to buy fresh corn from the farmers' market because it is picked that morning and is at peak quality. Bring it home, grill it, spice it up, and sink your teeth into the juicy, crunchy kernels.

¼ cup butter or ghee at room temperature

1 tablespoon salt

½ teaspoon hot chili powder

8 ears corn, husked and silk removed

2 tablespoons lemon or lime juice

Mix the butter or ghee with salt and chili powder, and make a paste.

Lightly spray the grates with cooking oil, then preheat the grill on high. Once it is hot, grill the corn for 10 to 15 minutes, turning every 5 minutes, until brown spots appear.

Once the corn is tender, remove from the grill and immediately baste with the spiced butter. Sprinkle the lemon or lime juice on the corn, and serve hot.

**Serves 6 to 8.**

# Mung Dahl with Chana Dahl  मुंग चना दाल

This a very versatile dish. The dahl can be served with rice or any Indian bread, or you can eat it as a soup. This is a very healthy, alkalizing, and nourishing dish for the body. When you want to eat light, this is a great option.

1 ¼ cups split mung beans

¼ cup chana dahl

1 tomatillo, diced small

1 serrano chili, sliced in half

2 tablespoons peeled and grated ginger

⅛ teaspoon fenugreek seeds (methi), optional

1 medium zucchini, diced and peeled

2 tablespoons ground coriander

1 teaspoon red chili powder

1 teaspoon turmeric powder

1 tablespoon salt (or to taste)

8–10 cups water

**Tempering ingredients (place each in separate small bowls)**

4 tablespoons ghee or oil

1 teaspoon cumin seeds

10 curry leaves

¼ teaspoon hing (optional)

1 tablespoon lemon juice

2 tablespoons chopped cilantro leaves

Add the mung beans, chana dahl, tomatillo, serrano chili, ginger, fenugreek (if desired), zucchini, coriander, red chili powder, turmeric, salt, and water to a pressure cooker.* Cook on medium for 10 to 15 minutes, or until the cooker whistles (follow your pressure cooker directions). Turn the heat off, but leave it on the stove to continue cooking with residual heat for another 20 to 30 minutes. Be patient and wait for the pressure to be released before opening the pressure cooker. At this point, it should slide open effortlessly.

Mash the hot dahl with a ladle or big spoon, or use an immersion blender, until it forms a smooth paste.

*Tempering the ingredients:* Heat the ghee or oil in a 4-quart saucepan on high. Once the ghee is hot, add the cumin seeds. When the seeds start to pop, add the curry leaves and hing (if desired).

Immediately add the tempered spices to the dahl paste, and mix thoroughly. If the dahl is too thick, add water to create the desired consistency. The dahl tends to thicken as it cools.

Add the lemon juice and mix well. Garnish with cilantro.

**Serves 6 to 8.**

*This dahl can be cooked on the stove if a pressure cooker is not available. Other methods require soaking the beans overnight and take longer to cook (see Dahl Chart on page 12).*

# Cucumber Raita ककड़ी रायता

**Raita is a staple for every dish. It balances spicy heat and heavy dishes with cooling qualities.**

3 English cucumbers, peeled and grated

1 ½ teaspoons salt (divided)

5 cups plain yogurt

½ teaspoon red chili powder

¾ teaspoon roasted cumin powder (or try Bina's Roasted Cumin)

1 tablespoon chopped cilantro leaves

Place the cucumbers in a colander, add ¾ teaspoon of the salt, and allow to sit for 5 minutes. Squeeze the excess water from the cucumber. If the water is not squeezed out, it will dilute the yogurt.

In a large bowl, mix the yogurt and cucumber together. Add the remaining ¾ teaspoon salt, the chili powder, cumin, and cilantro, and mix well. Refrigerate until ready to serve.

**Serves 6 to 8.**

# East Indian Coleslaw  कोबी सब्जी

My guests always rave about this twist on coleslaw. It can be served as a vegetable or cold salad with a bite. I love its crunch. Do not overcook this vegetable after tempering—take it off the stove immediately.

1 medium green cabbage, finely shredded

1 carrot, finely shredded or grated

1 teaspoon salt

**Tempering ingredients (place each in separate small bowls)**

¼ cup vegetable oil

1 teaspoon black mustard seeds

1 serrano chili, diced, with seeds

5 curry leaves (optional)

Pinch of hing (optional)

3 tablespoons lime juice

2 tablespoons finely chopped cilantro leaves

Mix the cabbage, carrot, and salt in a bowl.

*Tempering the ingredients:* Heat a deep 12-inch skillet, and add the oil. When the oil is hot, add the mustard seeds. While the seeds are popping, add the serrano chili, curry leaves (if desired) and hing (if desired). Immediately add the cabbage mixture. Turn off the heat. Stir to coat the vegetables with the spice mixture. Do not overcook. Leave it crunchy.

Squeeze the lime juice over the vegetables before serving, and mix well.

Garnish with the cilantro. Serve hot or cold.

**Serves 6 to 8.**

# Bina's Yellow Potatoes पीला अलू सब्जी

My family and friends gave the dish this name because it's a favorite of everyone who has eaten them. In my home, it was called *batata*, which means potato, and *nu shaak*, which means vegetable. Use it as a breakfast side dish or as a side dish with any of your favorite proteins. You can also make this with sweet potatoes or butternut squash for a twist.

2 medium potatoes (any kind)

2 teaspoons turmeric powder

1 tablespoon salt (or to taste)

1 ½ tablespoons ground coriander

2 teaspoons red chili powder

**Tempering ingredients (place each in separate small bowls)**

⅓ cup vegetable oil

1 teaspoon black mustard seeds

Pinch of hing (optional)

½ teaspoon sugar (optional)

1 tablespoon lime juice

2 tablespoons chopped cilantro

Peel and dice the potatoes, and place in a bowl.

Measure the turmeric and salt in a small bowl. Measure the coriander and chili powder in a separate small bowl.

*Tempering the ingredients:* Heat the oil in a 4-quart saucepan on high. When the oil is hot, add the mustard seeds. While the seeds are popping, add the hing (if desired). Add the potatoes and turmeric-salt blend. Mix well until the potatoes are coated. Reduce the heat to medium, cover, and cook for 10 minutes, stirring halfway to prevent potatoes from sticking to the bottom of the pan.

Add the coriander-chili powder blend and mix well. Cover and cook for another 3 to 5 minutes. When the potatoes are done, add the sugar (if desired) and lime juice, and mix gently.

Garnish with the cilantro and serve.

**Serves 4 to 6.**

# Seekh Kebabs सिख कबाब

These quintessential quick bites are available at roadside cafes, food carts, and restaurants. In a nutshell, they are highly spiced hot dogs made with ground meat that is skewered and grilled with herbs and aromatics. In India, the meat is threaded on long skewers and cooked in tandoors. The high heat of the tandoor sears the meat outside, making it crunchy, and locks in the juices inside. This popular appetizer is served with cilantro, mint chutney, naan, and onions—and is especially good with my Mint Mango Chutney (recipe on page 198). You can adjust the heat of this dish to taste by using fewer serrano chilies.

1 bunch cilantro leaves

1 bunch mint leaves

3–4 serrano chilies

15 cloves garlic

1 piece of ginger (1 inch long), or 3 tablespoons grated ginger

1 1/2 tablespoons salt

1 1/2 tablespoons amchur powder

1 1/2 tablespoons ground coriander

1 tablespoon poppy seeds

1 1/2 tablespoons roasted cumin powder (or try Bina's Roasted Cumin)

1 tablespoon ground white or black pepper

1 tablespoon red chili powder

1 1/2 tablespoons garam masala (or try Bina's Garam Masala)

4 pounds ground beef (85% lean) or lamb (91% lean) or a mixture of both

1 tablespoon club soda

Lime slices

Onion slices

In a blender or food processor, place the cilantro, mint, serrano chilies, garlic, and ginger. Grind and set aside.

In a medium bowl, mix the salt, amchur powder, coriander, poppy seeds, cumin, pepper, chili powder, and garam masala. Set aside.

Put the meat in an extra-large bowl, and add both spice mixtures. Blend well with your hands. Add the club soda. Make large balls with the meat (2–3 inches), and thread them on bamboo skewers. Shape all the meat into large hot dogs.

Spray the grates with cooking oil, then preheat the grill on high for 15 minutes. Turn the burners to medium. Place the kebabs horizontally, an inch apart from each other. Close the grill and cook for 3 minutes. Turn the kebabs one-third of the way, and repeat until cooked to desired doneness.

Remove from the grill and garnish with lime and onion slices.

Serve with Green Cilantro Chutney (recipe on page 200) or Mint Mango Chutney (recipe on page 198) and naan, flatbread, or hot dog buns.

**Serves 10 to 12.**

*Serve with a raw salad made with sliced red onions, 2–3 quartered limes, and 6 serrano chilies.*

# Watermelon Juice तरबूज़ का रस

Summer is the season for watermelon, and no 4th of July barbecue would be complete without it. This recipe is so easy, delicious, and refreshing, you will want to make it all summer. Enjoy this thirst-quenching drink on a hot day. I like to add a bit of lychee juice to it sometimes, for a nice variation. Watermelon Juice is very good for the lymphatic system.

1 seedless watermelon

3 cups ice cubes

10 mint leaves

Cut the watermelon in half and then in quarters. Cut several vertical slices every 2 inches through each wedge to the bottom of the rind. Then make several horizontal slices across the wedge to make cubed pieces. To release the cubes, cut horizontally just above the rind along its curve, all the way across. Measure 8 cups of cubes.

In a blender, add the watermelon cubes and ice cubes. Blend until smooth.

Pour into clear glasses, garnish with mint leaves, and serve.

The word *chatni* comes from the Hindi verb *chaatna* meaning "to lick"—and chutneys are lip-smacking, finger-licking delicious! India is obsessed with chutneys, relishes, and pickles, and each household has its own unique variation and combination. As a result, there is a staggering variety of chutneys. While relishes are sweeter, chutneys tend to be pungent and hot and have a much shorter shelf life than relishes and pickles.

Chutneys are condiments that are an essential accompaniment in Indian cuisine, and not only brighten a bland meal, but also bring zest, sparkle, and punch to a spicy one. They whet appetites, facilitate digestion, and add a finishing touch to any meal. Traditionally, chutneys were ground on stone; today, we have the luxury of food processors and blenders that make chutneys quick and easy to prepare.

In this chapter, I share my favorite chutneys. One ingredient dominates the flavor of each, reflected in the chutney's name. Coconut Chutney (recipe on page 202) pairs well with idlis and dosas. I like to serve the Mint Mango Chutney (recipe on page 198) with grilled meats. The sweet and sour Amchur Chutney (recipe on page 199) and Date and Tamarind Chutney (recipe on page 201) are served with savory snacks such as pakoras, samosas, pani puri, aloo chat, and potato pattice with chole. There are no rules for chutneys—they can stand alone or be served together because of the range of flavors. They all complement each other.

These are a few suggestions of my favorites. Be adventurous, and put one in your chicken salad, on your vegetable tray as a dip, or alongside your spicy meat and vegetable dishes. I love to make a grilled chutney sandwich with my favorite fillings. They can be mixed and matched and used in many ways, so have some fun with these!

# Chapter 11

# Chutneys

Cashew Chutney with Cilantro     198

Mint Mango Chutney     198

Green Pecan Chutney     199

Amchur Chutney     199

Garlic Chutney     200

Green Cilantro Chutney     200

Date and Tamarind Chutney     201

Coconut Chutney     202

# Cashew Chutney with Cilantro काजू धनिया चटनी

Did you know that powdered cashews are a great thickener for soups and stews? They could be the perfect substitute in vegan dishes. My sister has a home in Goa, and there we visited the tropical spice plantations where cashew trees are abundant. I had fun creating this chutney with its large, beautiful cashews. I use this as a salad dressing and a dip, but it is also fabulous as a gravy for vegetables or pasta, potato pattice, or crab cakes. This chutney can be made many days ahead of time. However, it thickens in the refrigerator; you can dilute it with water or broth to desired consistency.

1 cup raw cashews

1 bunch cilantro leaves

2–3 serrano chilies (optional)

1 tablespoon lime juice

1 cup water

¾ tablespoon salt

¼ teaspoon sugar

Add all the ingredients to a blender or food processor, and grind to a smooth paste. Place in a decorative bowl and serve.

# Mint Mango Chutney फुदीना आम चटनी

My husband is very fond of creating pickles and chutneys. This recipe is his concoction, and it is simple to make and goes with everything. We serve it with Seekh Kebabs (recipe on page 192) and savory snacks. On Sundays, we eat sandwiches, and this goes in our paninis as a spread. He's very proud of this recipe, and my entire family savors this chutney.

1 large bunch mint leaves

¾ bunch cilantro leaves

1 green mango peeled, pitted, chopped (unripe mango should be firm)*

1 1-inch piece of jaggery or 1 tablespoon brown sugar

3 green onions with tops

1 teaspoon roasted cumin powder (or try Bina's Roasted Cumin)

1 tablespoon salt

2 or 3 serrano chilies

1-inch piece of ginger (peeled)

Put all the ingredients in a food processor, and grind to a chunky consistency.

Serve with kebabs, savory snacks, or my street food menu in Chapter 3.

*Note: If the mango is not sour enough, add ¼ lime with skin on to the blender.

# Green Pecan Chutney हरी पिकोन चटनी

I drew inspiration from my friend Usha to create this chutney. She now lives in Atlanta, Georgia, which is famous for its pecans. Pecans are not native to India. This recipe is fantastic as a dip for raw vegetables of your choice and can be served with any of my savory snacks. It tastes especially good with my Mung Dahl Bhajias (recipe on page 174). A couple of tips: If you plant whole coriander seeds, you'll get cilantro. Also, a pinch of baking soda will keep greens green.

3 large bunches cilantro leaves

1 lime, juiced (2 tablespoons)

2–3 serrano chilies

1 teaspoon cumin seeds

1 tablespoon salt

¼ teaspoon sugar

1 cup water

1 cup pecans

Pinch of baking soda

Add all the ingredients to a blender or food processor, and grind to a smooth paste.

Serve with an assortment of raw vegetables, pasta, or Potato Pattice (recipe on page 152).

# Amchur Chutney आमचुर चटनी

Amchur is a dried mango powder and is a souring agent. The chutney has complex flavor combinations of sweet, sour, and pungent—three of the six Ayurveda tastes. This is a great accompaniment to Chole (recipe on page 161) and Potato Pattice (recipe on page 152). It's delicious served with Bombay street foods and other savory snacks. This chutney also goes well with my Green Pecan Chutney (above).

½ cup amchur powder, sifted (dried mango powder)

3 cups water

1 cup sugar

2 teaspoons red chili powder

2 teaspoons roasted cumin powder (or try Bina's Roasted Cumin)

1 ½ tablespoons salt

In a medium pot, mix together all the ingredients and cook on high for 4 to 6 minutes, until the mixture boils. Reduce the heat to medium.

Stir every 3 minutes for the next 11 minutes, until the sugar melts, the dry ingredients are well incorporated, and all lumps disappear. The liquid will reduce to 2 cups. Remove from the stove and allow the mixture to cool to room temperature.

Cover and chill in the refrigerator for 2 hours before serving. As it cools, it will turn into the consistency of a thick paste.

# Garlic Chutney लहसुन चटनी

There's no hiding the distinct aroma of garlic wafting through your open windows, which may cause neighbors to pay you a visit and ask, "What are you cooking?!" Garlic is delicious as well as highly nutritious, with amazing health benefits. Research has shown garlic boosts the immune system, reduces the chances of getting the common cold, combats high blood pressure, and lowers cholesterol. It also keeps Dracula away!

10 cloves garlic

1 tablespoon sea salt flakes

½ teaspoon red chili powder

1 tablespoon ground coriander

Press the garlic in a garlic press, and add to a small bowl with the salt, chili powder, and coriander.

The chutney can be stored in the fridge for up to 10 days.

Sprinkle over toasted and buttered buns, or serve with Vadaa Paav (recipe on page 68).

# Green Cilantro Chutney हरी धनिया चटनी

Cilantro and coriander come from the same plant. Cilantro is the leaves of the planted coriander seed and goes by many names, such as Chinese parsley and Mexican parsley. This chutney is called dhania chutney in India because *dhania* means "coriander" as well as "cilantro." It's a great accompaniment for any vegetable, meat, fish, or snack. This nutritious herb is used in many ways, including for garnishes, chutneys, pastes for vegetables, and smoothies—which becomes a power drink, thanks to cilantro's blood-cleansing qualities.

2 bunches cilantro leaves

½ cup pecans or walnuts

1–3 serrano chilies*

1 teaspoon cumin seeds

2 tablespoons lime juice

¾ tablespoon salt

¼ cup fresh coconut (optional)

½ cup water (divided)

In a blender, place the cilantro, nuts, serrano chilies, cumin seeds, lime juice, salt, and coconut (if desired) with ¼ cup of the water. Blend until smooth, adding just enough of the remaining water to form a thick paste. Add a bit more water if needed.

*The number of serrano chilies used will adjust the heat to taste.

# Date and Tamarind Chutney खजूर इमली चटनी

The best dates come from the Middle East, a product of the desert. Fresh medjool dates are common in India because they are brought from the Middle East. Full of natural sugar, dates are a healthy way to satisfy a sweet craving. Dates rejuvenate and revitalize your system when you're tired and exhausted—great for grounding vata. This chutney is usually served with Pani Puri (recipe on page 65) and Mung Dahl Bhajias (recipe on page 174), but it's versatile enough to use with many recipes.

1 cup water

1 cup pitted dates

¼ cup tamarind paste*

1 tablespoon salt

1 teaspoon red chili powder

In a small pot, bring the water to a boil. Add the dates and allow them to boil for 1 minute, or until soft.

In a high-speed blender, combine the dates and their water, tamarind paste, salt, and chili powder. Blend until smooth.

Refrigerate until use.

**Serves 6 to 8.**

*Tamarind paste is available in Asian and Indian grocery stores.*

# Coconut Chutney नारियल चटनी

This chutney is served with all South Indian meals. Use frozen coconut from Kerala (see Frequently Asked Questions, page 208), which is affordable and available in the frozen section of Indian grocery stores. Buying coconut frozen guarantees freshness and quality.

1 bag (14 ounces) frozen shredded unsweetened coconut

2 serrano chilies

¼ cup chana, roasted and dried (optional)

1 tablespoon lime juice

1 ½ tablespoons salt

1 cup water (as needed)

**Tempering ingredients (place each in separate small bowls)**

2 tablespoons vegetable oil

½ teaspoon mustard seeds

8–10 curry leaves

1 whole dried red chili

¼ teaspoon split urad dahl (or white dahl; see Dahl Chart on page 12)

⅛ teaspoon hing

**Optional**

½ cup plain yogurt, or juice from half a lemon or ½ cup coconut milk yogurt (for dairy-free options)

In a blender, combine the coconut, serrano chilies, chana (if desired), lime juice, salt, and a little of the water. Blend until smooth, adding just enough water to blend the ingredients. (Too much water will make the mixture too thin.)

*Tempering the ingredients:* Heat the oil in a small saucepan. When the oil is hot but not smoking, add the mustard seeds and cook until the seeds start to pop. Remove from the stove and quickly add the curry, dried chili, urad dahl, and hing. Add to the coconut mixture and stir.

*Optional:* For a creamier chutney, add the yogurt (pictured), or the lemon juice or the coconut milk yogurt to the coconut mixture and stir.

# Frequently Asked Questions (FAQs)

### In a nutshell, what is Ayurveda?

It's India's ancient system of medicine and lifestyle that offers guidelines for happy, harmonious living. Rooted in a 5,000-year-old tradition and steeped in the wisdom of the six systems of Hindu philosophy, it addresses the holistic health of mind, body, and spirit. It also provides a profound knowledge of the structure of the universe: that we are all interconnected. When Ayurveda was revealed to the sages long ago, their homes were in forests, mountains, and caves, which connected them intimately to their surroundings.

Ayurveda is a system of inclusion. We human beings are part of a whole grand scheme, which is our universe. It teaches us to constantly seek balance and alignment with mind, body, and spirit in an ever-changing world. It is about adaptation and flexibility with everything and everyone around us—environment, career, relationships, family, friends, elements, universe, and God. Ayurveda teaches us to seek harmony in our entire being, in both the outer (our physical bodies) and the inner (our soul and spirit). These need to be in balance to live joyfully and in peace and to ensure disease-free, radiant health.

### Is Ayurveda a vegetarian diet?

No. Ayurveda is an ancient holistic lifestyle approach that does not exclude any food groups. Ayurveda merely states that there is a time, place, season, and reason when we must be flexible with our food choices because life is evolutionary. Ayurveda recommends meat for certain body types at certain times in their lives as needed. For more about body types, see "About Ayurveda" on page v.

### What is the difference between curry, curry plant, and curry leaf?

There is confusion around these three terms—and for good reason! One little word refers to three unrelated things.

The term *curry* was invented by the British when they colonized India. And while it's commonly thought of in the United States as a spice powder found on grocery store shelves, in India it means something entirely different. There, curry is a generic term for any dish with a sauce and a unique combination of many spices. In every region of India, the spice blends vary depending on what is available, the season, and the household preferences. Masala and curry are interchangeable terms.

The curry plant, or *helicrysum*, is indigenous to the Mediterranean region in Italy. It has linear, silver-gray leaves that are curry scented. This plant is not recommended for eating or spicing food, but can be used for potpourri and making essential oils.

The curry leaf, with the botanical name *Murraya koenigii*, is native to India. It is commonly known as sweet neem or kari patta, and is an essential ingredient in South Indian recipes such as sambhar, rasam, and coconut chutney. The bright-green leaves grow to about 2 to 4 inches and are bitter and very fragrant. The leaves are highly valued as seasoning in southern and west coast Indian cooking and also for their medicinal value.

### Which products do you recommend, and where do I find them?

To expedite the cooking of Indian food, I have found a few shortcuts and good products that make the process easier and faster but also maintain the authentic flavor. I have used Patak's mild or hot curry paste in tandoori chicken, spinach saag, and chicken makhani, and this product is readily available in grocery stores. MTR rasam masala and sambhar powder are products I have tested repeatedly and been extremely happy with.

Whole Foods, Sprouts, and Natural Grocers carry many ingredients required in Indian cuisine in their ethnic aisles. Indian grocery stores—found in most cities—are a great resource for all the ingredients, pastes, and powders I use in my recipes. If they don't carry an item, they are usually willing to order it for you, and they're very inexpensive. Of course, you can order almost anything online. At home, I shop at India's Rice 'n' Spice in Fort Collins, Colorado.

### What is turmeric?

Turmeric, an herb and a spice, has been used in India for thousands of years and is the root of a plant related to ginger. It is indispensable in an Indian pantry. Its bright golden-orange color—leading to its nickname "saffron of India"—gives curries, vegetables, eggs, tea, and milk an attractive hue. Its taste is bitter, pungent, and astringent, so it needs to be used sparingly.

Science recently affirmed what the ancient Indians already knew about the benefits of turmeric for healing and well-being. Turmeric contains a compound called curcumin, which helps fight and reverse diseases. Now, turmeric has set the world ablaze with its ability to help heal chronic and debilitating diseases with no adverse effects. It's no surprise that it's becoming a popular remedy for just about anything that ails you. Its benefits include: anti-depressant, anti-inflammatory, anti-flatulence, arthritis management, blood purifier, cholesterol treatment, diabetes management and prevention, liver cleanser, hypertension, inflammatory bowel disease, insomnia, kidney and thyroid issues, natural pain killer, and a natural approach as a preventive, and it stimulates digestion.

You can add turmeric powder to recipes, buy turmeric in capsule form, or make Golden Milk Elixir (recipe on page 133) to drink. Turmeric is available in all grocery stores, but East Indian markets carry this fresh as a rhizome and a powdered golden spice form. Wear gloves when chopping the root because it stains easily.

## How do I prepare ginger?

Ginger is a rhizome or root like turmeric, cream colored inside. I peel fresh ginger with a potato peeler, then grind it in a small food processor and save the paste in a glass jar for making chai or adding to my vegetables, lentils, and meat. It helps to have this prepared ahead of time. For best results, use the ginger paste within five days.

## Where can I find saffron at a decent price?

Saffron is best bought at an Indian market or specialty Persian store, as it is usually cheaper and fresher than a chain grocer. It is an expensive spice but has innumerable health benefits. Ask for the saffron at checkout as it is not displayed on shelves in ethnic markets—it is often kept behind the counter. The price of saffron varies because of its demand and supply. I buy Spanish Saffron or Kashmir Saffron in a 1-ounce tin, since I use a sufficient amount of saffron in my preparations. I find it economical to buy a larger quantity. I love cooking with saffron since it has a fabulous aroma and delicious taste—and the orange glow rendered in the food is extremely appetizing. I use it to make desserts, vegetables, rice, pasta, tea, meats, and more.

## How do you recommend organizing the needed spices to speed up the cooking process?

A typical Indian kitchen houses the most commonly used spices in a stainless steel box with seven mini containers that hold 2 to 4 ounces of spices. It is called the spice garage or masala dabba. *Masala* means "spices," and *dabba* means "box." If you cook Indian cuisine frequently, then a masala dabba will make cooking easy, quick, and extremely efficient.

I have two masala dabbas with my frequently used spices. In one box, I have red chili powder, turmeric powder, ground coriander, black mustard seeds, cumin seeds, garam masala, and roasted cumin powder. I have tiny spoons in each container that is powdered. In the second box, I have cinnamon sticks, black cloves, black peppercorns, red chilies, green cardamom pods, black cardamom pods, and fennel seeds. I keep the masala dabba on the left side of the stove in the top drawer, for easy access when I am cooking. Also, when I'm tempering, I don't have to fumble to find my spices.

## Should I use a pressure cooker, slow cooker, or Instant Pot?

These three small appliances help make one-pot meals such as soups, stews, lentils, and meat. All three offer convenience and ease in cooking, but have distinct functions and separate sets of cooking instructions.

In India, a pressure cooker is a necessity in the kitchen. It is convenient because the contents can be cooked in between 5 and 20 minutes. Our lentils and beans cook within minutes, and entire meals can be ready in a jiffy. The cooker creates steam from the water added to the contents and builds up pressure as it is heated, which expedites cooking and locks in nutrients.

If heated for too long, though, the food can sometimes turn into mush. Once you get accustomed to using a pressure cooker, it is easy to use. I love it and cannot do without it.

If you prefer a slow cooker, it cooks just as good as a pressure cooker, but you will have to plan ahead. On low heat, it will take anywhere from 6 to 10 hours for the food to be done.

The new Instant Pot is amazing since it can be a pressure cooker, stir-fryer, or a slow cooker. The key is to learn its nuances, what works for you, and what's most comfortable.

## Should I use canned or fresh tomatoes?

I like to use fresh produce whenever I can since Ayurveda teaches to live in rhythm with nature. When tomatoes are vine-ripened and in season, they are delicious, juicy, colorful, and fun to cook with. In winter, I find the tomatoes are hard—because they are ripened in a hothouse or greenhouse—and the taste is lost. This is when I resort to canned tomatoes. I especially like the San Marzano and Hunt's fire-roasted tomatoes that are crushed or small diced. Any of your favorite brands will work, but choose the ones without basil and oregano. Also, fresh tomatoes tend to be expensive, so the canned ones offer a suitable alternative to keep you within your budget.

## Which salt should I use?

That's a million-dollar question. There are hundreds of salts from every country to choose from. I stock gray salt, rock salt, black salt (sanchal), and Himalayan salt, and I choose from among these in recipes that call for salt. It is important to know that all salts have different intensities, so keep this in mind when using your favorite. According to Ayurveda, rock salt balances and pacifies all three doshas. Salt is a combination of two elements, water and fire. While it has cooling, oily qualities of water, it can also be heating because it whets your appetite. Salt is also one of the six tastes essential in an ideal Ayurvedic diet.

## Which kind of rice should I use?

Hundreds of varieties of rice are found throughout the regions and climates of India. Rice is a gluten-free staple, especially in South India where there are rice paddies everywhere. It is more of a shorter grain and a little stickier than basmati rice, which predominantly grows in the foothills of the Himalayas and Punjab. Basmati is a fragrant long-grain rice that is now available everywhere. In my South Indian recipes for idlis and dosas, my preference is using long-grain white rice for soaking, grinding, and fermenting the batters. In my North Indian menus, I like to use the Kohinoor and Dawaat brands of basmati rice because they have a slender, aromatic, extra-long grain that showcases my biryanis and rice pilafs beautifully. There are others that are just as good—you cannot go wrong.

### How do I retain the green color of boiled green vegetables?

It may be an old wives' tale, but I was told by my grandmother and mother to add just a pinch of baking soda to the cooking water when boiling or cooking green vegetables such as green beans, peas, and spinach. Doing this maintained the vibrant green color produced by the plant pigment, chlorophyll. These greens produce organic acids, which reduce the pH level of the water. Baking soda helps to alkalize and neutralize these acids in vegetables. More than a pinch of baking soda will overcook vegetables and ruin the taste. A little goes a long way!

### Where do you find coconut products in nontropical regions?

Coconut is native to the beautiful coastal region of Kerala, where coconut palms dance and sway with the ocean breezes. This is also the home of Ayurveda, where it all began. Kerala literally means "land of coconut trees." Coconut is considered a sacred symbol of prosperity and a gift to this land. This multipurpose tropical fruit with a hard, nutlike shell has high economic and medicinal values.

Cooking with coconut products is easy these days, since they are readily available in local grocery stores. They come in different forms, such as sweetened and unsweetened dried coconut flakes, canned coconut milk, and organic coconut oil. The product I like the most is the unsweetened coconut that comes from Kerala and is available in the frozen section of Indian grocery stores in the United States. Instead of trying to grate your own coconut, which is not easy, this is a simple and inexpensive alternative—it is already prepared and ready to use. Making my coconut-based dishes and chutneys are really easy with this product.

# Glossary

**Aachari**
Pickled and salted relishes, meat dishes, and vegetables that can be made sweet or hot, depending on the blend of spices.

**Ajwain**
Also called carom seeds. A spice that looks like miniature cumin seeds with an aroma similar to thyme. It is not caraway seeds. It has a bitter and pungent taste. Use sparingly because it tends to dominate a dish.

**Akuri**
The Indian version of scrambled eggs, but never overcooked (slightly runny). The main flavoring is small-diced green onions and serranos, grated ginger, and finely chopped cilantro; it's garnished with sliced tomato and roasted cumin powder.

**Aloo**
The Hindi word for "potatoes."

**Amchur**
A fine beige powder made of dried green mangoes. It is used as a souring agent or a meat tenderizer in Indian cooking. Available in Indian food markets.

**Arrowroot**
A gluten-free starch obtained from the root of tropical plants and processed into a fine white powder. It is useful as a thickening agent for sauces and a binding agent for vegetable patties. It should be first mixed with a cold liquid to form a slurry and then added to the dish to be thickened. Arrowroot has a more neutral flavor than cornstarch and tends to break down more easily when heated. Arrowroot should not be combined with dairy products as it can produce an unpleasant texture.

**Bay leaf**
The aromatic dried leaf of the bay tree used to impart its flavor during the cooking process and then removed from the dish before consuming.

**Besan**
Also known as gram flour, this is a yellow flour made from ground Bengal gram or chickpeas. Gram flour has an added bonus of being gluten-free. It has a nutty flavor and is used as a thickener in curries, as well as in batters, dumplings, sweets, and breads.

**Bhajias (or pakora)**
A savory Indian dish made with a spiced besan batter and deep-fried like tempura. Bhajias can be made with chopped vegetables or meat.

### Bharta
An Indian dish of roasted eggplant often cooked with onion, tomato, and grated ginger, then mashed with pungent spices. Sometimes yogurt is added.

### Bhel
Commonly sold as a snack on the streets of Mumbai. Bhel is a savory, crunchy salad made of puffed rice, crispy chickpea noodles called sev, vegetables (such as onions, potatoes, and raw green mangoes), a tangy tamarind sauce, garlic chutney, and cilantro chutney. It also has sprouted mung and small black chickpeas.

### Biryani
An Indian version of lasagna with rice as the base, layered with sauce and meat, fish, or vegetables. Heavily influenced by Persian royal tables, this dish can contain luxuries such as saffron, raisins, and nuts.

### Black chana
Also known as Bengal gram, these chickpeas come from India where they are sun-dried until they turn a deep rust color. Like regular chickpeas, they have a deep, earthy aroma and a nutty flavor. They contain a great deal of protein and fiber and are also ideal for sprouting. Black chickpeas can be found in Indian markets and specialty food shops.

### Black pepper
The best black pepper is the tellicherry. In the state of Kerala, along the Malabar coast in India, the pepper vines flourish and thrive. The famous tellicherry pepper of this region is considered the "queen of peppers." The British discovered this humble spice in 1600 when they colonized India, and now this is a staple spice in every household worldwide.

### Boil
Cooking term used to describe heating water to 212 degrees at sea level. The temperature lowers by 2 degrees for each 1,000 feet of altitude. The boiling point is reached when bubbles are consistently breaking the water's surface in the pot.

### Bundi
A snack food made from sweet or savory fried besan. The batter can be mixed with spices, fried, and eaten on its own or soaked in water and added to yogurt as a side dish.

### Burfi
A dense, sweet, milk-based dessert from India.

## Cardamom

Dry green pods full of sticky, tiny black seeds that have a sweet flavor and pungent aroma. Ground cardamom loses flavor quickly, so use pods, whole or crushed. There are two main types of cardamom: green and black. Green is the most common used as a flavoring and spice in both food and drink, and has a medicinal value. Cardamom is also known as the queen of spices.

## Chaat masala

A spice blend typically consisting of amchur, cumin, coriander, dried ginger, black salt, black pepper, asafetida, and chili powder. It is typically served on a small plate to be sprinkled on food as desired.

## Chana dahl

Small, roasted split chickpeas that look very much like yellow split peas. They are one of the oldest legumes (or pulses) known to mankind and are popular in India, Pakistan, Afghanistan, Europe, northern Africa, and Mediterranean countries. Chana are high in protein and are sold in Indian stores.

## Chapatti

An unleavened flatbread staple from India also known as roti.

## Chole or chana

A cooked dish of white chickpeas or garbanzo beans with great health benefits. Chole is a staple of Punjab (North India), served as street food alongside a bread called puri.

## Chutney

Generic name for sauces or relishes made with fruits or vegetables, herbs, lime juice, spices, or sugar. There are several varieties and combinations of chutneys, which are accompaniments for meats, snacks, and breads.

## Cilantro

An herb grown from coriander seeds. It is a colorful garnish and also used for many chutneys in Indian preparations. Buy them in bunches of fragrant green leaves.

## Cloves

The dried, unopened flower buds of the clove tree. Brown and nail-shaped, they have a pungent flavor, so use (whole or ground) in moderation for flavoring.

## Coconut

The fruit of a coconut palm. The inner nut is encased in a husk that must be removed. The hard shell can then be drained of juice and cracked open to extract the white meat. Coconut meat is jelly-like in younger nuts and harder in the older ones.

## Coconut milk

Coconut milk and coconut cream are both made from grated coconut meat that is soaked in hot water; the cream is skimmed off the top, and then the remaining liquid is squeezed through a cheesecloth to extract a white liquid that is coconut milk. The milk is different from coconut water, which is the unprocessed liquid from within the coconut. Coconut milk is available in many varieties and brands in grocery stores.

## Coconut milk powder

A fine, white powder used in Southeast Asian and other cuisines. The powder is made from raw unsweetened coconut cream and is reconstituted with water for use in recipes that call for coconut milk.

## Coriander seeds

The round seeds of the coriander plant. The seeds have a spicy aroma, are widely used in Indian cooking, and are common in spice mixes such as garam masala. To intensify the flavor, dry-roast the seeds until aromatic, then grind them to a powder to flavor vegetables, lentils, and meats.

## Cumin seeds

Peppery, slightly bitter seeds that are very aromatic. To intensify the flavor, dry-roast the seeds, then grind them to a powder to flavor eggs, fish, meat, vegetables, and lentils.

## Curry

A generic term for any dish with a sauce and a unique combination of many spices. Also called masala.

## Curry leaves

Small green aromatic leaves native to India and Sri Lanka. The leaves have a distinctive flavor and have many underlying health benefits.

## Dahl

A generic term in India for dried split pulses such as lentils, peas, and beans. The term is also used to refer to the various soups prepared from these pulses. Dahl is often accompanied by roti, rice, and vegetables.

## Daikon

A mild-flavored winter radish with a long, white root. Very popular in Asian cuisine.

## Dhansak

A popular traditional dish served with rice containing a mix of lentils, vegetables, spices, and meat (often mutton or goat). It combines elements of Persian and Gujarati cuisines.

## Dosa

A type of pancake made from a fermented batter containing rice and split urad dahl. Dosas are a staple of South India, a favorite of every breakfast buffet, and a popular street food. It is gluten-free and dairy-free.

## Dosha

The five elements (earth, water, fire, air, and ether) that are organized in our bodies as three energetic principles called vata, pitta, and kapha. These govern function and structure in the body.

## Dudhi

Indian squash with a hard, light-green skin that should be peeled before consuming. Its pungent flavor with its biting-hot, sharp, and cumulative lingering effect and strong fruity aroma is great for seasoning in limited amounts.

## Dundicut peppers

Also known as Dundicut peppers or Asian red chili. They are dried red chilies (a variety of capsicum) that tend to be really spicy. Dundicut peppers' pungency is measured at 30,000 to 65,000 units on the Scoville scale. They are sold dried.

## Eggplant

Actually a fruit! Choose eggplant that are long, slender, deep purple, firm, and shiny, which have the least amount of bitterness and aren't quite so seedy; thus, they have a sweet, earthy flavor. Avoid eggplants that are bulbous or more round as they're more seedy, fibrous, and bitter.

## Fennel seeds

Oval, greenish-yellow seeds used as an aromatic and a digestive. They have a licorice taste. To intensify the flavor, dry-roast the seeds before crushing them.

## Fenugreek

See "Methi seeds."

## Fermentation

The process in which a substance is broken down into a simpler substance for the body to absorb easily. For thousands of years before refrigeration, ancient people understood the benefits of fermented foods. They aided digestion and nutrition, and fermentation also helped preserve food. Dosas and idlis are made with a fermented batter of rice and split urad dahl.

## Garam masala

A spice mixture in Indian cooking. In Hindi, *garam* means "hot," and *masala* roughly translates as "a mixture of spices." It is used alone or with other seasonings for enhancing flavors. Many versions of these are available.

### Ghee

Clarified butter made from the milk of a buffalo or cow and used in Indian cooking. Ghee can be heated to a high temperature without burning. According to Ayurveda, this is a vegan product.

### Ginger

The rhizome of a tropical plant, sometimes referred to as a root. Fresh young ginger should have a smooth, goldish skin and be firm and juicy. Ginger is also available dried and ground.

### Gujarati

A language and region of western India. Many Gujarati dishes are distinctly sweet, salty, and spicy simultaneously.

### Gulkand

A sweet preserve of rose petals from the Indian subcontinent. Gulkand is an Ayurvedic tonic with a multitude of health benefits.

### Hariyali

Typically, a mix of any green vegetables, such as spinach, swiss chard, mustard greens, and green peas.

### Hing

An amber-colored flavoring that comes from fennel-like plants, with an extremely pungent smell, earning it the nickname "devil's dung." Only a pinch is required. Also known as asafetida, hing is used in place of garlic and onions and is mainly used when tempering ingredients. It has medicinal benefits, including acting as a balancing condiment for digestion.

### Idli

A savory cake made by steaming a batter of fermented black lentils and rice. It is a staple of South India that has become popular all over the world because of its health benefits.

### Jaggery

A raw sugar with a caramel flavor, made from cane sugar. Jaggery is slightly sticky and varies in color depending on the juice from which it's made. Jaggery can also refer to palm sugar. Soft brown sugar can be used as a substitute.

### Kadhai

A wok for deep-frying.

### Kadhi

A spicy Indian dish with vegetable fritters called pakoras and thick yogurt gravy made from chickpea flour. It is served with sour yogurt. Kadhi is a great accompaniment for khitchdi.

**Kalonji seeds**
Small, teardropped-shaped black seeds, also called Nigella seeds. They taste like a combination of onions, black pepper, and oregano. They're used as a spice in North Indian cuisine and also as a garnish for naan.

**Karam podi**
A spicy powder mix made with spices, chilies, and lentils and served as an accompaniment for idlis and dosas.

**Khao suey**
A coconut soup served as a street food. This is India's adaptation of a Burmese ramen bowl. It contains egg noodles, vegetables, meat, and coconut milk.

**Khitchdi**
A meal made with rice and lentils that is eaten for cleansing, detoxing, or recovering from illness or surgery. A watered-down version is typically fed to Indian babies as their first solid food. Also known as kitchari.

**Macchi**
A generic name for "fish."

**Makhani**
Means "with butter" or "cream" in Hindi. This preparation is often used in North Indian dishes.

**Masala**
Any number of herbs and spices mixed and ground into a paste or powder to form a blend. Many different combinations can make a blend.

**Massoor**
Known in the American market as lentils. These whole lentils come in two colors—a deep brown and green. When split, they are salmon in color. The split ones are the most common as they cook more easily and don't usually need soaking like the whole ones do. Other names for these lentils are matki and bagali.

**Methi leaves**
Also known as fresh methi or fenugreek leaves. The leaves of young fenugreek plants, stripped off the tough stalks, are used as a vegetable and treated much like spinach. They have a mildly bitter flavor. The leaves are available fresh or dried in Indian food markets.

**Methi seeds**
Also known as fenugreek seeds, used as a spice in preparing pickles, vegetable dishes, dahls, and spice mixes. They are often roasted to reduce bitterness and enhance flavor. Use with discretion in lesser amounts because the bitterness can overpower a dish. These little seeds boast huge health benefits. When planted, we get methi leaves.

### Monk fruit sweetener

Sweetener extracted from a small, round fruit known in Chinese medicine called han gua. It has a sumptuous taste of sugar with no aftertaste and has zero calories and zero glycemic index. The Buddhist monks in the Luohan region of China discovered this fruit in the 13th century and cultivated it for reducing weight gain and aiding coughs and colds, and for increasing chi or prana, hence earning the name "immortal fruit" because it increases longevity.

### Mung bean

I use whole mung beans for sprouting. Split and skinned mung beans that are pale yellow in color are used for making dahl. Whole mung beans must be soaked before sprouting.

### Mustard oil

A strongly flavored oil made from pressed brown mustard seeds and used in Bengali, Punjabi, and North Indian cooking. The oil is usually preheated to its smoking point and then cooled to temper its strong aroma.

### Mustard seeds

Yellow, brown, and black mustard seeds are used in Indian cooking, especially in Bengal. Brown and black are interchangeable. The seeds are either added to hot oil to pop or are ground to a paste before use, making a spicy dry mustard. Dijon mustard and yellow mustard are made from mustard seeds. Huge fields of these yellow-flowered plants are found in northern India, and saag made with fresh mustard greens is a staple in this region.

### Naan

A type of leavened bread served in Indian cuisine typically in a teardrop shape. This bread is traditionally cooked in a special clay oven called a tandoor.

### Okra

Eaten as a vegetable and used to thicken soups and stews. When cut, okra releases a mucilaginous substance that disappears during cooking. It is also known as bhindi or "ladies' fingers."

### Paav bhaji

A popular street food from Mumbai, consisting of a thick vegetable curry usually prepared in butter or ghee and served with a soft bread roll.

### Pakora (or bhajias)

An Indian savory dish made with a spiced besan batter and then deep-fried. Bhajias ("fried vegetables") can be made with chopped vegetables or meat and is like a Indian tempura.

### Paneer

A fresh cheese made by coagulating milk with lemon juice or vinegar and leaving it to drain. Paneer is usually pressed into a block and refrigerated. It is available in Indian food markets.

### Pani puri
A round puffed pastry that is filled, fried, and dunked in a spicy flavored water. The filling is a mixture of spiced mashed potatoes, sprouted chana and mung, and chutney. It is a popular street food.

### Paratha
A flat, thick piece of unleavened bread fried on a griddle or tava and can be stuffed with vegetables or eaten plain.

### Pattice
A potato patty either stuffed with peas or plain. It can be served with chole and is a common street food.

### Puris
A small, round, flat piece of bread made of unleavened flour, deep-fried and served with meat, lentils, or vegetables and yogurt.

### Raita
An Indian side dish of yogurt containing chopped cucumbers or other vegetables and spices.

### Rajma
Also known as kidney beans. It is best to soak them overnight before cooking. Rajma dahl is the Indian version of red beans and rice and is eaten with rice, roti, or naan.

### Rasam
A thin, very spicy South Indian soup served alone or combined with other foods, such as rice, idlis, or dosas. It is an excellent cold remedy.

### Rice flour
A flour sometimes mixed with spiced besan to make bhajias or pakoras. It can also be mixed with mung dahl bhajias to make them crunchier.

### Saag
A generic term for leafy greens like spinach, mustard greens, collard greens, basella, etc. This is a favorite dish often eaten with rice or bread such as roti or naan. It is sometimes served with paneer.

### Saffron
Considered the "king" of the spice world, extremely flavorful with numerous health benefits. The strands give an intense orange-yellow color when cooked with rice and have a powerful aroma. Only a few strands are needed for each dish. It must be soaked in liquid before use. The red stigmas are considered the pure saffron.

### Sambhar

A lentil-based vegetable stew served with idlis and dosas. It is a typical dish from the south of India. Sambhar is a generic name for dahl.

### Samosa

A savory pastry filled with spiced potatoes and peas and fried in oil. Its size and consistency may vary, but typically it is triangular or tetrahedral in shape. Indian samosas are usually vegetarian and often accompanied by a mint and date chutney. They have gained popularity all over the world.

### Semolina

A fine, coarse, or medium grain made from processed wheat with the wheat germ removed. It swells when cooked, to give a creamy, textured effect. It is commonly known as "cream of wheat." It's used for sweets and upma.

### Serrano

A type of fresh chili pepper that originates from the mountainous regions of Mexico. It is medium-hot in flavor.

### Shrikhand

A sweet dish made of strained yogurt. It is one of the main desserts in Gujarati cuisine. It tastes like ambrosia and contains saffron and cardamom.

### Tamarind

A souring agent made from the pods of the tamarind tree. Its sweet but tart edible pod-like fruit is also a legume used as the base for all sorts of savory dishes, stews, and condiments. It is available as a fresh tamarind or as a prepared puree or concentrate.

### Tandoori

A clay oven that delivers a very distinct flavor only achieved in this appliance. It is used to make many dishes, such as kebabs, chicken, naan, and kulchas. (In the story of Ali Baba, when he was chased by the king's guards, he hid in a big clay pot turned upside down—a tandoor!) There is now a tabletop gas oven tandoor available in the United States.

### Tempering process

A seasoning process (also called tadka) used in Indian cooking. Spices and aromatics are fried in oil, and then the flavored oil is stirred into the dish, most commonly at the end of cooking. This is a finishing process that blends the flavors of all the ingredients together.

### Thandai

A healthy cold drink that is a mixture of almonds, fennel seeds, rose petals, black pepper, cardamom, saffron, milk or water, sweetener, and other spices. It is an excellent drink for a hot summer day.

### Toovar

Also called yellow lentils, these come oiled and plain. Oiled ones look slightly greasy and need to be soaked in hot water to remove the oil before cooking. Toovar are also known as pigeon peas.

### Turmeric

The root of a plant related to ginger, sold either dried and ground or fresh like gingerroot, but orange inside. The herb has a slightly bitter flavor and a pungent aroma. It is used for color, fragrance, and flavor, and also for its immense health benefits.

### Upma

An Indian-style savory "cream of wheat." It is used as a breakfast item in India and is occasionally served with vegetables and spices.

### Urad

A small-seeded black pulse resembling the related green mung bean. Also called "whole black gram," urad can be found split or whole. When husked, the urad dahl is white inside. The split urad dahl is used when making dosa and idli batters, and it becomes glutinous and creamy when cooked.

### Vadaa paav

A deep-fried potato patty served in a bun like a hamburger with cilantro chutney and garlic chutney. A popular vegetarian fast-food dish, it originated as cheap street food in Mumbai and is now offered in stalls and restaurants throughout India.

### Whey

The liquid remaining after milk has been curdled and strained in the paneer-making process. Whey can also be made by straining yogurt.

### Yogurt

A food produced by the bacterial fermentation of milk. Fermentation by these bacteria—known as yogurt cultures—produces lactic acid, which acts on milk protein to give yogurt its texture and characteristic tart flavor. Cow's milk is commonly available worldwide and, as such, is the milk most commonly used to make yogurt.

# Index

(Recipes in bold)

Achari, 210
    **Achari Aloo** (Mustard Potatoes), 22, **37**
Ajwain, 20, 210
Akuri, 210
    **Akuri Scrambled Eggs with Cilantro and Ginger**, 148, **153**
Amchur, 3, 20, 210, 212
    **Amchur Chutney**, 195, 196, **199**
Ayurveda, iv, v, vi, ix, x, 10, 16, 37, 41, 44, 75, 111-112, 115, 129, 199, 204, 207-208, 215

Besan (chickpea flour), 12, 20, 57, 68, 70, 118, 122, 210-211, 217-218
Bhajia: see Pakora

Bharta, 21, 211
    **Roasted Eggplant Bharta**, 22, **32**
Biryani, 91, 99, 102, 207, 211
    **Bina's Chicken Curry for Biryani**, 92, **94**
    **Biryani Rice**, 92, **96**
    **Raita for Biryani and Dhansak**, 92, **99**
    **Vegetable Biryani**, 92, **98**
Breads, 2, 16, 21, 50, 107, 210, 212
    **Chapatti** (Unleavened Bread), 164, **168**
    **Masala Puri**, 42, **44**
    **Naan**, 22, **39**
    **Pani Puri**, 60, **65**
    Roti, 16, 19, 21, 27, 87, 129, 168, 212-213, 218
Burfi, 210
    **Coconut Burfi** (Kopra Pak), 130, **145**

Cardamom, 3-7, 20, 75, 206, 212, 219
Chai, x, 20-21, 44, 59, 73, 147, 163, 206
    **Authentic Indian Chai**, 60, **73**
Chana: see Chole
Cheese: see Paneer
Chicken, 21-22, 59, 90-91, 99, 103, 126, 129, 177, 180, 195, 205, 219
    **Bina's Chicken Curry for Biryani**, 92, **94**
    **Chicken Tikka Masala**, 22, **26**
    **Hariyali Chicken Kebabs**, 60, **64**
    **Indian Fajitas**, 178, **180**
    **Tandoori Chicken**, 22, **23**
Chickpeas, 11-12, 20, 27, 65, 155, 158, 210-212
Chole, 12, 59, 152, 161, 195, 199, 212, 218
    **Chole** (Garbanzo Beans) 148, **161**
Chutney, 48, 57, 64, 78-79, 147, 152, 174, 195-196, 205, 208, 211-212, 218-220
    **Amchur Chutney**, 196, **199**
    **Cashew Chutney with Cilantro**, 196, **198**
    **Coconut Chutney**, 196, **202**
    **Date and Tamarind Chutney**, 196, **201**
    **Garlic Chutney**, 196, **200**
    **Green Cilantro Chutney**, 196, **200**
    **Green Pecan Chutney**, 196, **199**
    **Mint Mango Chutney**, 196, **198**
Cilantro, 7, 20, 196, **198**, **200**, 210-212, 220

Cinnamon, 3-7, 20, 206
Coconut, 20, 26, 75, 147, 195-196, 205, 208, 212-213, 216
    **Coconut Burfi** (Kopra Pak), 130, **145**
    **Coconut Chutney**, 196, **202**
    **Coconut Kadhi**, 112, **118**
    **Delightful Cashew Coconut Curry**, 112, **120**
    **Khao Suey** (coconut soup), **126**
Coriander, 3-5, 20, 75, 129, 206, 212-213
Corn, 177
    **Corn Khees**, 42, **48**
    **Grilled Spiced Corn**, 178, **181**
Cream of Wheat; see also Upma, 61-62, 148, **159**, 219-220
Cumin, x, 3-7, 20, 206, 210, 212-213
Curry, 3, 7, 20, 41, 75, 91, 129, 204-205, 213, 217
    **Bina's Chicken Curry for Biryani**, 92, **94**
    **Chettinad Curry**, 76, **90**
    **Delightful Cashew Coconut Curry**, 112, **120**
Curry paste, 20, 23, 26, 29, 94-95, 98, 205

Dahl (lentils); see also Glossary, 2, 11-13, 16, 20, 21, 41, 129, 147, 212-214, 216-220
    **Karam Podi**, 76, **89**, 216
    **Maa Ki Dahl** (Black Dahl), 22, **27**
    **Massoor Dahl with Spinach**, 130, **140**
    **Mung Dahl**, 112, **121**
    **Mung Dahl and Spinach**, 42, **45**
    **Mung Dahl Bhajias**, 13, 17, 164, **174**
    **Mung Dahl Dosa**, 76, **79**
    **Mung Dahl with Chana Dahl**, 178, **184**
    **Rajma Dahl**, 164, **175**
    **Sambhar** (recipe), 76, **86**
    **Trevti Dahl** (Three Mixed Dahls), 112, **128**
Dahl and Rice Chart, 12
Deep-frying, 16-18
Detox, i, vi, 3, 10, 13, 52, 111, **114**, **119**, **128**, **129**, **216**
Dhansak, 213
    **Dhansak**, 92, **103**
    **Raita for Biryani and Dhansak**, 92, **99**
Dosa, 13, 16, 75, 147, 195, 207, 214, 216, 218-220
    **Mung Dahl Dosa**, 76, **79**
    **Potato Filling for Dosa**, 76, **87**
    **Traditional Dosa**, 76, **78**
Dosha, **v-vii**, 10, 129, 204, 207, 214
Drinks: see also Milk
    **Authentic Indian Chai**, 60, **73**
    **Green Power Drink with Kale and Cucumber**, 112, **119**
    **Watermelon Juice**, 178, **193**

Eggplant: see Vegetables
Eggs
    **Akuri Scrambled Eggs with Cilantro and Ginger**, 148, **153**
    Hard-boiled eggs, 95

Fenugreek, 3, 20, 75, 214 216
Fermentation, 13, 75, **79**, **82**, 214, 220
Five elements, iii, v, x, 214

Garam masala: see Masala, x, 3, 206, 213, 214
Garbanzo beans: see Chole

Ghee (clarified butter), 5-7, **9-10**, 18, 215

Hing, 215

Idli, 13, 59, 75, 147, 195, 207, 214, 216, 218-219
    **Idli** (Steamed Rice Cakes), 76, **82**

Kadhi, 215
    **Coconut Kadhi**, 112, **118**
    **Gujarati Kadhi**, 112, **122**
Kapha, v, vii, 10, 79, 82, 115, 214
Khitchdi, 111, 129, 215, 216
    **Khitchdi** (recipe), 112, **114**

Lamb: *see* Meat

**Macchi** (Fish) 130, **141**, 216
Masala, x, 3, 20, 204-206, 212-214, 216
    **Chicken Tikka Masala**, 22, **26**
    **Masala Puri**, 42, **44**
Massoor: *see* Dahl
Meat; *see also* Chicken
    **Baby Rack of Lamb**, 164, **166**
    **Seekh Kebabs**, 178, **192**

Milk: *see also* Drinks
    **Chaash**, 112, **116**
    **Golden Milk Elixir**, 130, **133**
    **Thandai Spiced Almond Milk**, 92, **110**, 219

Mung beans: *see* Dahl

**Naan**; *see* Breads

Oils (cooking), 5-7, 17-18, 20, 75, 208, 217, 219

Pakora: *also called* bhajia, 12, 59, 195, 211, 215, 217-218
    **Mung Dahl Bhajias**, 13, 17, 164, **174**
    **Paav Bhaji**, 60, **71**
    **Pakora**, 42, **57**
Paneer, 2, 14, 21, 217, 220
    **Paneer** (Indian Fresh Cheese), 22, **36**
    **Paneer Mutter** (Cheese and Peas), 22, **33**
Puri, 16, 41, 59, 147, 195, 218
    **Masala Puri**, 42, **44**
    **Pani Puri**, 60, **65**
Paratha, 16, 19, 147, 218
    **Paratha Stuffed with Radish**, 148, **150**
Pitta, v, vii, 10, 79, 82, 115, 214
Potatoes, 147, 177, 210, 218-219
    **Achari Aloo** (Mustard Potatoes), 22, **37**
    **Bina's Yellow Potatoes**, 178, **189**
    **Potatoes and Peas**, 42, **49**
    **Potato Filling for Dosa**, 76, **87**
    **Potato Pattice**, 148, **152**
    **Vadaa Paav**, 60, **68**
    **Potato Raita with Hot Mustard**, 92, **107**

Raita, 6, 91, 129, 147, 218
    **Bundi Raita** (Chickpea Flour Snacks in Yogurt), 22, **38**
    **Cucumber Raita**, 178, **185**
    **Eggplant Raita**, 112, **123**

    **Fresh Mint and Green Onion Raita**, 164, **167**
    **Fresh Mint Raita**, 92, **99**
    **Potato Raita with Hot Mustard**, 92, **107**
    **Raita for Biryani and Dhansak**, 92, **99**
    **Spinach and Zucchini Raita**, 42, **53**
    **Yogurt**, 112, **115**
Rasa, iii, iv, 2
Rice: *see also* Idlis, 11-12, 16, 20, 21, 41, 75, 91, 111, 116, 129, 207, 211, 214-216, 218
    **Biryani Rice**, 92, **96**
    **Caramelized Rice**, 92, **106**
    **Eggplant Rice**, 164, **171**
    **Fragrant Saffron Basmati Rice**, 130, **137**

Saag: *see* Vegetables
Salad, 41, 147, 211
    **Black Chana Salad**, 148, **155**
    **East Indian Coleslaw**, 178, **188**
    **Mango Pomegranate Salad**, 130, **144**
    **Raw Salad**, 92, **102**
    **Sprouted Mung Salad and Dressing**, 130, **136**
    **Vitamin Bhel Salad**, 148, **158**
Sambhar: *see* Dahl
**Samosa**, 59, 60, **61**, 195, 219
Sattvic, 115
**Shrikhand**, 42, **56**, 219
Soup, 213, 217
    **Coconut Kadhi**, 112, **118**
    **Gujarati Kadhi**, 112, **122**
    **Khao Suey** (coconut soup), 112, **126**, 216
    **Mung Dahl and Spinach**, 42, **45**
    **Rasam**, 76, **83**, 218
    **Sambhar**, 76, **86**
    **Trevti Dahl** (Three Mixed Dahls), 112, **128**
Spice conversion chart, 5
Sprouting, 2, 11-12, **65**, **136**, **155**, **158**, 211, 217

Tamarind, 3, 20, 75, **201**, 211, 219
Tandoori Chicken; *see* Chicken
Tempering, 2, 5-7, 19, 206, 215, 219
Turmeric, 3, 20, 129, 205-206, 220

**Upma** (Indian Cream of Wheat), 148, **159**

Vata, v, vii, 10, 79, 82, 115, 201, 214

Vegetables: *see also* Potatoes
    **Bina's Okra**, 164, **170**
    **Butternut Squash**, 130, **132**
    **Caramelized Onions**, **106**
    **Cauliflower and Peas**, 42, **50**
    **Eggplant Raita**, 112, **123**
    **Eggplant Rice**, 164, **171**
    **Green Beans**, 42, **52**
    **Potatoes and Peas**, 42, **49**
    **Roasted Eggplant Bharta**, 22, **32**
    **Saag** (Spinach), 22, **29**

Yogurt; *see* Raita, 13, 20, 41, 111, 112, **115-116**, 129, 147, 215, 218-220

# Acknowledgments

When I took on the writing of this book, I did not realize I needed a large team to support this venture. I give my deepest thanks to all who have helped with this monumental undertaking so selflessly and to friends and family who believed in and encouraged me. Without their help and insight, I would not have been able to complete this project. It has been an enormous undertaking, and I am deeply grateful for everybody's help and guidance to bring my vision and my inspiration to life. Specifically, I would like to thank:

Rajiv, my husband, who has assisted me by wishing the best for me and supporting me financially and emotionally. He tries to fulfill everything I desire. He is always challenging me and urging me to be the best that I can be.

Kabir, my son, whose fire, strength, and passion inspired me to write my cookbook. I will never forget when he said, "Mom, if you don't write your cookbook, all your delicious recipes will be lost." He assists me with his advice in understanding how to run a company and how to motivate people working for me. Most of all, he taught me how team building works and how to be a leader.

Mona, my daughter, who many years ago gave me the courage to incorporate my business, Methi Masala. She helped with my digital marketing and website, and now I am finally using them.

Phyllis Quinn, my dear friend for many years, a published cookbook author and chef extraordinaire, whose advice on recipe development and cooking processes has been invaluable to me. She is always there for me whenever I need her.

Robert Nardozza, my ballroom dance coach and partner for the last 20 years, who has always believed in me and supported me with my dreams. He would always tell me, "You can do it. If anyone can, you can," especially when challenges arose.

Elizabeth, Karina, and Anna who kept my company's momentum going by identifying priorities, assigning tasks, and keeping this project on track.

Jane Barber, project manager, who helped me complete the production of this project with focus, organization, and support. She coordinated every aspect of the production of the manuscript and marketing plan.

Susan Hindman and Samantha Prust, editors who helped me polish my prose, keeping my voice true.

Laura Birlingmair, my designer, who produced a beautiful book using Harper Point's amazing professional photography.

Karel Waltermire, my friend, who assisted me with developing and testing my spice blends.

Sasha, who assisted me with marketing materials and my professional storefront.

Nancy Plemmons, Kerri Abbott, Leslie, Yessenia, and Kenny, and all the other recipe testers who helped me hone my instructions to make them the best recipes possible.

For all those not mentioned, I am truly grateful for everything you've done. I could not have completed this venture without you.